SUPERMAN
ON THE COUCH

SUPERMAN
ON THE COUCH

What Superheroes Really Tell Us about Ourselves and Our Society

DANNY FINGEROTH

Foreword by STAN LEE

continuum

NEW YORK • LONDON

2004

The Continuum International Publishing Group Inc
15 East 26 Street, New York, NY 10010

The Continuum International Publishing Group Ltd
The Tower Building, 11 York Road, London SE1 7NX

Printed in the United States of America

Library of Congress Cataloging-in-Publication Data

Fingeroth, Danny.
    Superman on the couch : what superheroes really tell us about
ourselves and our society / Danny Fingeroth ; foreword by Stan Lee.
        p.   cm.
    Includes bibliographical references and index.
    ISBN 0-8264-1539-3 (alk. paper)—ISBN 0-8264-1540-7
(pbk. : alk. paper)
    1. Comic books, strips, etc.—Psychological aspects.   2. Comic books,
strips, etc.—Social aspects.   I. Title.
PN6714.F54   2004
741.5'9—dc22   2003020893

For Varda, Ethan, and Jacob

CONTENTS

FOREWORD
by STAN LEE

The public's interest in superheroes never seems to wane.

Most of the books written about those ubiquitous costumed crusaders always tend to deal with their origins and exploits.

But this one is different.

Author Danny Fingeroth, with more than twenty-five years' experience as a highly regarded, professional comicbook writer and editor, attempts to learn why people have been deeply involved with superheroes for so many years. He digs beneath the surface to discover the reasons for the ever-growing appeal of these costumed cavorters, in whatever medium they may appear. And, as a surprising extra bonus, he delves into the extremely pertinent question—what does the perennial popularity of superheroes tell us about our own society's needs and values?

But don't let those high-sounding topics throw you off. Danny's approach is neither dry nor pedantic. You're going to find that this book is fun, just as the whole superhero mythos is fun. What's more, you'll explore subjects very few writers have tackled before, topics that may make you reconsider preconceived notions and perhaps bring you greater appreciation of the superhero stories you've always enjoyed.

It's doubtful that you can find a better guide than Danny himself when he brings you his insightful analyses gleaned from a long and respected career as a pro—a pro who has, for years, been intrigued by the worldwide appeal and amazing longevity of fictional superheroes. The conclusions he reaches will both surprise and fascinate you as he colorfully demonstrates that superhero writers and artists, like all creative people in every medium, have always, with surprising accuracy, reflected our society and the times we live in.

Having researched and digested volumes of information on this topic, Danny presents it in his own unique and informal manner. Once you gratefully get past this inevitable introduction, you'll begin to glean a much greater understanding of why superheroes have captured the imaginations of people of all ages.

I've no desire to give away the many surprises that are in store for you on the pages ahead, but here is just a small sample of the topics that will amuse and entertain you, and best of all, will make you think . . . .

- What is there about the human condition that makes superhero tales so compelling to us?
- Why must we constantly reinvent the more-than-human heroic ideal?
- What is there about characters such as Spider-Man and Batman that have enabled them to transcend their original comicbook origins and become international movie and TV stars?
- What do superheroes tell us about our own interpersonal relationships?
- How have superheroes helped create our society's values? How have the superheroes themselves been shaped by those values?

- Why are so many superheroes orphans?
- What is the real meaning of the superheroes' secret identities?

With that, I'll leave you in the capable hands of Danny Fingeroth who's about to take you on a lively, literary fun ride, giving you new and exciting ideas to titillate you, just as the best superhero stories themselves do.

Whether or not you agree with Danny's conclusions, after you've reluctantly turned the very last page, I'm sure you'll never look at superhero fiction the same way again.

Excelsior!

1

WHY SUPERHEROES?

I am lying in bed counting sheep when all of a sudden it hits me. I conceive a character like Samson, Hercules, and all the strong men I have ever heard tell of rolled into one. Only more so. I hop right out of bed and write this down, and then I go back and think some more for about two hours and get up again and write that down. This goes on all night at two-hour intervals, until in the morning I have a complete script.

Jerry Siegel, co-creator of Superman

WHEN Jerry Siegel recalled his teenage experience of creating his first version of Superman, in what can only be called a Herculean night of inspiration and execution, he succinctly described what it is that we find so compelling about these heroes of modern myth.

That Siegel, in his official recounting of his own "creation myth," deliberately chose to reference Samson and Hercules is no accident. In connecting his creation to universally known and respected—if not necessarily admired—heroes of religion and mythology, Siegel tells us it's no accident that Superman and the myriad heroes inspired by him are seen as godly figures. This is most apparent in the comics adventures of the Norse thunder god Thor, whose incarnation as a superhero is a potent conflation of god and man.

To discuss superheroes, we must first establish what a hero is, as slippery a slope as searching for such a definition might be.

A hero can be said to be someone who rises above his or her fears and limitations to achieve something extraordinary. In the real world, firemen who race into burning buildings, soldiers who advance in the face of enemy fire, astronauts who launch into space despite the high odds of lethal outcome, are often the standard by which heroism is measured.

On another level, still in the world we inhabit, a teacher who, day after day, attempts to educate under adverse circumstances, an accident victim who, despite pain and enormous difficulty, persists in relearning lost skills, or a physician who ministers to AIDS patients in a plague-stricken, third world nation can all be considered heroes. They fight the odds, and sometimes beat them.

Indeed, do we not all, at one time or another, as the alarm clock rings and we steel ourselves to face another day in the struggle that life can be, regard ourselves—even as we laugh at the assessment—as heroes of our own lives? There are days when simply taking the subway or freeway to work and getting through that day seems like the triumph of Gilgamesh, or the Green Lantern, for that matter.

A hero embodies what we believe is best in ourselves. A hero is a standard to aspire to as well as an individual to be admired. This is true for those we deem heroes in the world around us . . . and it is true, but in different ways, for the *fictional* heroes we encounter in prose, theater, and on screens of various types and sizes.

While many face each day as a struggle, there are those people who wake up with a song on their lips and a smile on their faces as they eagerly rush to their assigned tasks. We simultaneously admire and despise such people. You know—much the way we feel about, say, Superman's arch-nemesis, Lex Luthor. You just *know* that Luthor enjoys his life. He spends his time doing what we sometimes, in our darkest, secret moments, would like to be doing: plotting—and executing—revenge against his enemies.

Wait! We're not supposed to like him. He's the "bad guy."

But as a *fictional* villain, he's safe to fantasize being. You can enjoy pretending to be Luthor in a way most people wouldn't allow themselves to fantasize about being Hitler or Attila. Luthor isn't real. His murders are all in the imagination. The enormity of his crimes and the ruthlessness of his worldview—as can also be said of his fellow comic book evildoers such as the Joker, Magneto, the Green Goblin—actually help *define* the comic book hero. And at the end of the day, the (usually) triumphant hero part of our imaginations forgives us for identifying with—or at least enjoying—the villain as much as the hero.

So there are real life heroes. There are fictional heroes. (There are even sports "heroes" and music "heroes," but the term, when used this way, generally refers to someone we like, who excites us, but not necessarily someone who has exhibited selfless bravery in the face of near-impossible odds and life-threatening possible consequences.) But have we really arrived at a definition of heroism yet? Let us continue.

There are, and have always been, *fictional* heroes. Sam Spade. Philip Marlowe, Sherlock Holmes, come to mind. These individuals, though imaginary, are putatively human. But are they heroes? Or are they simply *compelling protagonists* that we can relate to? Is Michael Corleone a hero? Not by most standards. But he is certainly the character we identify with and root for in *The Godfather* book and movies. Interestingly, both versions are careful to point out that Michael was a decorated hero of World War II. These are the human fictional heroes. They could be one of us, if we really worked hard to maximize our potential.

Biblical and mythological heroes are clearly precursors of super-heroes. Odysseus, Thor, Moses are individuals of courage, commitment and noble ideals, flawed though they may be as individuals.

Somewhere in the evolution of the fictional hero, a subset of the heroic figure came to be possessed of *superhuman* qualities. It came to be under-stood that the hero was defined by *fearlessness*, as opposed to the ability to face and overcome fear. Skill was at the peak of human ability, but so was *luck*. At one point, the most popular genre in which these "special" people starred was the western. Buffalo Bill may not have been able to fly—but how many thousands of bullets passed harmlessly over and around him? If that's not magic, what is? Roy Rogers and Gene Autry shot and sang their way past all manner of danger. In the pulps and on the radio, the Shadow possessed mystical powers, which he came upon through hard work.

Doc Savage, The Shadow, Ka-Zar—these were the pulp heroes who preceded Superman and Batman. They all had elements of being seem-ingly reality-based, but were really creations of pure fantasy. Dirty Harry and Rambo are, theoretically, normal humans. But scratch them and you'll find tights and a cape not very far beneath the surface.

So, the question must be asked:

What Is a Superhero?

The realm of superheroes is occupied by individuals with fantastic powers (whether magic or "science" based), as well as people who fight their battles with advanced technology (often differentiated from magic only because the author says so) or people who are just plain brave/crazy/lucky. What, then, makes a character a superhero? What does the thunder god Thor have in common with the nighttime avenger, Batman?

Then most obvious things are: some sort of strength of character (though it may be buried), some system of (generally-thought-to-be) positive values, and a determination to, no matter what, *protect* those values. These are also, interestingly, the characteristics of a villain. And, as the saying goes, every decent villain thinks of himself as the hero. Hitler had no doubt that *he* was the good guy.

So somehow, the superhero—more than even the ordinary fictional hero—has to represent the values of the society that produces him. That means that what, say, Superman symbolizes changes over time. In the 1950s, he may have been hunting commies. In the 1970s, he may have been clearing a framed peace activist against a corrupt judicial system. Either way—the hero does the right thing. Perhaps more importantly, *he knows what the right thing is.*

As Richard Reynolds points out in his *Super Heroes: A Modern Mythology,*

> *Superheroes are by and large not upholders of the letter of the law; they are not law enforcement agents employed by the state. The set of values they traditionally defend is summed up by the Superman tag of Truth, Justice and the American Way. Sometimes the last term has been interpreted in a narrowly nationalistic way . . . but far more often . . . has stood for the ideals enshrined in the US Constitution.—74*

The superhero must also possess skills and abilities normal humans do not. This includes so-called normal heroes like Batman. Notwithstanding his virtual agelessness over six decades (while his sidekicks somehow grow and mature), Batman, on a daily basis, leaps—unarmed—into gunfire and mutant-powered muscle—coming out with nary a scratch. (His back once famously broken in the 1990s, he now is as good or better than new. Those Wayne family billions must've bought some very good physical therapy indeed.) As amazingly, Batman pretty much always knows *who* the guilty party is and just *how much* manhandling they require to be subdued. He may scare them witless, but he never hurts them more than he needs to. In itself, this, too, can be seen as an almost magical power. He even has the approval of the community—he is officially deputized by Gotham City—to smooth out any rough aspects of his perception by the public of his fictional universe.

One strain of superhero mythology comes from the same mythic impulse that spawned Paul Bunyon and John Henry. Clearly, these figures have powers beyond those of even the most highly skilled and expertly trained athletes. Yet, they do not come from distant planets or have super-soldier serum coursing through their veins. They are able to perform their superhuman acts of heroism through grit and determination. They do it—whatever *it* is—through sheer will.

One thing a superhero will usually *not* do, at least permanently, is die. John Henry proved that he could outdo the mechanical steel-driving machine, but proving so cost him his life. When Superman moves an asteroid out of a collision course with Earth, it may tire or deplete him for a time . . . but tomorrow, he'll be there to defuse Brainiac's latest threat to humanity.

Why Are Superheroes Important to Us?

There's no doubt that the superhero has became one of the staples of popular entertainment and, through that, of mass consciousness. Reflect on the following catchphrases found in our daily language:

"Who does he think he is—Superman?" may be asked about someone who takes on tasks and responsibilities above and beyond his powers or abilities.

"My spider sense is tingling," says the woman who suspects someone's motives.

"Don't Hulk out over this," an enraged kid is cautioned by his schoolyard tormentors.

"Riddle me this, Caped Crusader," one corporate executive will ask another as a preface to a tricky question in the course of a business meeting.

Superheroes are as taken for granted in our minds and metaphors that we rarely wonder how and why they came to be such important parts of our inner lives. Once one starts to explore, many questions come to mind.

Why do we need more than one superhero? Why was Superman able to spawn several generations of other heroes (including a 1990s hero *called* Spawn)? Why has a genre of characters that embody certain values, characters that were first created in the 1930s and 1940s, continued to resonate for us?

Why are superheroes important to us?

What is it about us that feels we have to invent these fantasy beings to rescue us? And what are they rescuing us from? Clearly, Superman and his friends did not beat Hitler, as many times as they may have trounced him in the pages of their magazines. Batman doesn't make us any safer when we walk the late night deserted streets of downtown. Or do we feel somehow that he is watching over us? Do we embody the Batman within us and take that next step in the darkness because that's what the Caped Crusader would do?

Moreover, why do we seem compelled to keep re-creating the superhero generation after generation?

When you think of Sherlock Holmes, you probably imagine a nineteenth century detective, solving cases that Scotland Yard of that era could not. When you hear the name the Lone Ranger, you immediately conjure an image of a masked gunman—a proto-superhero if there ever was one—riding the plains on his white horse, all set firmly in the 1880s.

But when you think of Superman, you most likely think of the Superman that was in vogue when *you* were a child. There's been a Superman for every decade since the character was created, as there has been a variety of Batmen, Wonder Women, and Spider-Men. And the medium you remember that character in could vary by the era, too.

Is the Superman you remember from the comic book? The TV series? The films? The radio show?

There is no "Moses for the 1940s," no "John Henry for the 1950s," no "swinging sixties Gilgamesh." Yet, superheroes keep being reinvented. The superheroes of the 1940s were re-imagined as the heroes of the 1960s, which exist to this day. They had the same names, often similar powers, yet otherwise bore no connection to them. But whatever the version, the Flash is fast, Aquaman rules the undersea world, the Martian Manhunter is still a space-alien detective.

But there's no Thin Man for the new millennium. There's no Sam Spade in space. There's no Lone Ranger riding a 4×4.

And newer superheroes are described in terms of the old ones. They're often hybrids.

Spawn? Batman and Spider-Man with a horror twist.

Savage Dragon? The Hulk with a fin on his head.

What is it about the classic comics superheroes that so enthralls us? Why does the *Buffy the Vampire Slayer* TV series constantly reference classic comics plots in its own story lines—with the characters often even discussing that they're doing it as they interact? Why do the rhythms of the spy thriller series *24* seem so familiar to us? Could it be because they echo the serial nature of comics—which themselves echo the continuing nature of 1930s and 1940s movie serials?

Further, the question must be asked: Is such preoccupation with these archetypes healthy for an individual or a society? Is our love of these heroic types an abnegation of our responsibility to confront the problems we face individually and collectively? Are we living in some dream world, unwilling or unable to face up to our real adversaries and stumbling blocks?

Do superheroes provide an image of "friendly fascism"? Is the very idea that they know when and how to do the right thing inherently instilling a misguided sense of dependence on authority in those who partake of the fantasies? Is a society that idolizes a Superman one that will fall prey to a myth of an Aryan *Übermensch*? Will the vigilante certitude of Batman that he is doing the right thing lead Batman fans to take the law into their own hands, each becoming his or her own Commissioner Gordon, condoning our own—or our designated Batmen and women's—right—and duty—to kick butts and take names on our behalf? Will the catharsis provided by the good feelings engendered by the racial tolerance metaphor of the X-Men's struggle for acceptance lull us into complacent acceptance that racial struggles for change have gone as far as they need to?

Do superheroes provide us with super-excuses?

Or, conversely, do these superhuman, ultimately moral (in some certain way that we ourselves can rarely be) beings provide us with a healthy fantasy outlet for our own darker sides? Does Wolverine rip into his enemies so that we can be more understanding of those who oppose us in daily life and societal relations? Does his violence make ours unnecessary? Don't even the most open-minded and forgiving of us long to see someone who's done something "bad" get their comeuppance— and in a violent, direct, blunt manner?

Do superheroes provide us with a respite from having to be perfect ourselves, even while inspiring us to aspire to greater levels of achievement and good works? Can we emerge from the fantasy world they provide and go on to do more and better deeds in our own? Can we emerge from that fantasy world and go about our business, feeling that—at least in some corner of our consciousness—revenge has been served, hot and bloody, not cold and reasonable? Can we assimilate the better parts of these heroes' moral codes without incorporating the less attractive parts of their behavior and modes of operation?

Interestingly, it has been decades since psychiatry or psychology has taken a critical look at such questions about superheroes. In the 1940s and 1950s, when comic books in general, and superhero comics in particular, were riding as high as they ever would, Dr. Benjamin Spock, the baby doctor to the parents of the baby boomers, in his *The Common Sense Book of Baby and Child Care,* opined that even violent action-comics were basically harmless to children.

It was psychiatrist Fredric Wertham, the most well known of the critics of the medium and the genre who beat the drum most loudly against comics, focusing on crime comics but also encompassing superhero magazines. (Others who shared his negative views of comics included social critic Marya Mannes and folklorist Gershon Legman.) Wertham, a reform-minded progressive who was responsible for many positive changes in the psychiatric care system, believed in societal, as opposed to individual, responsibility for social problems, especially the postwar scourge of what was called "juvenile delinquency." This perceived rise in the quantity and brutality of crimes committed by children and teenagers was seen by Wertham and others as stemming from a popular culture that numbed children to the effects of violence, racism, and sexism. For whatever reasons—perhaps because the comics industry was less formidable than the movie or TV industries—Wertham attacked comics and lobbied to have them censored for children, though not for adult readers. While stating that virtually all violent young offenders were readers of crime comics, Dr. Wertham was certainly no great fan of the superhero. In his 1954 book *Seduction of the Innocent,* as quoted by Mark Evanier in his ironically titled *Wertham Was Right* (TwoMorrows, 2003), he famously put forth the notions that Batman and Robin sharing a mansion as Bruce Wayne and Dick Grayson ". . . is like a wish dream of two homosexuals living together," and that: "the homosexual connotation of the Wonder Woman type of story is psychologically unmistakable." In an era when homosexuality was still considered a mental illness, clearly this was no compliment.

Other experts took the position that comics were actually good for children. As noted by Amy Kiste Nyberg in her 1998 *Seal of Approval: The History of the Comics Code*, in 1941 psychiatrists Lauretta Bender and Reginald Lourie "described comic books as modern folklore, noting that the omnipotent superheroes had their parallels in fairy tales; replacing magic with science was simply expressing basic ideas in contemporary terms."

But the voices of comics's attackers were heard more loudly by parents and teachers desperate for an easy explanation for the growing problem of youth crime that became pronounced in postwar society.

There is, however, little written in recent decades by mental health professionals about superheroes. There is much literature about fairy tales and mythology, including works by Bruno Bettelheim, Rollo May, C. G. Jung, and Joseph Campbell, but no major specific studies of superheroes by psychiatrists or psychologists. Perhaps, over the years, the superhero has become entangled in the cacophony of popular culture inputs that surround us on all sides. One of the aims of this book is to see just how the superhero has become part and parcel of modern pop culture, how it influences and is influenced by other genres and subjects.

Perhaps the nonreligious context of the superheroes makes them perfect for a multireligious society like ours. After all, to make a superhero out of Jesus or Buddha or Vishnu would suddenly make the heroic adventure highly partisan. And whereas there are superheroes who are specifically religion-based, these are most often clearly used to instruct or to proselytize, with entertainment as a means to these ends.

A "my god can beat up your god" type of conflict is precisely what people go to popular culture to *escape*. Although Judeo-Christian comics creators have indeed made superheroes out of the Norse, Greek, and Roman godly pantheons—Thor and Hercules, for example are popular superheroes—the handling of these characters is decidedly *secular*. The pantheons each of these heroes come from are treated more like alien races than agglomerations of deities. Again, the lines between the supernatural and science are blurred, to useful effect.

So, along with our other modern religion-substitutes—psychoanalysis, political *isms,* celebrity worship—we now have the "cult" of the superhero. Of course, since this cult seems to extend to the general populace of the planet, perhaps, in some strange way, the superhero is more influential than any one religion or substitute. In the most optimistic view, maybe the superhero can even unite people across ethnic, religious, and national boundaries. Again, the sheer box-office success of superhero films around the world is a sign this may be true.

I explore these and other relevant issues in this book. A society, like a family, lives by a series of myths it tells itself over and over. A grandfather may tell you again and again of his long years of bitter struggle to achieve present-day success, knowing full well that you have heard the story over and over again. But he knows his listeners love to hear the stories repeated, and that each telling is received at a different time in the listener's life, and with different meaning gleaned from each hearing. The family bond is reaffirmed with each telling and listening. In a similar manner, we collectively tell ourselves the same sorts of stories in the guise of entertainment. In the end, good will triumph over evil. When we hear a story where that is not the case, it may resonate as truer to life . . . but no longer qualifies as inspiring entertainment. Modern heroes may more often win ambiguous or qualified victories, one could say that simply surviving the evil that surrounds a fictional hero qualifies as some sort of victory.

One could call the superheroes' never-say-die attitude the idealized vision we have of ourselves and our society. But, in reality, it is the idealized vision the entire world has of itself. As discussed earlier, no one thinks of himself or herself as the bad guy. As writing teacher Robert McKee says in his book *Story:* "Attila does not question the rightness of his pillaging, raping, and plundering. It is what he does. No doubt he believes that by doing it, he is doing good."

In the pages that follow, I shall explore the origins of the heroic myth, and how this came to become the superhero myth of American and British popular culture. I'd like to convey a sense of some of the energy and creativity that led to the formation of the pop-culture icons that have lasted for the better part of a century, and have blossomed from—but certainly never cut the ties with—the comics medium.

As a comics reader and lover, and as a professional writer and editor of comics for a quarter of a century, I have deep and complex feelings about the medium and the characters it has spawned. As I write or help others in the creating of their stories, there is, of course, just the need to "feed the machine" and make a deadline, the ever-regenerating deadline. But there is also a conscious feeling of responsibility: how will this small brick in the edifice that is pop culture affect coming generations? The answer, generally, is "very little," or "not at all." But, of course, one never knows. Will a character created to serve a need ("We need to create a hero with Internet powers—whatever that means.") and meet a deadline end up becoming the next iconic demigod of the comics medium? Will it find its fame in a comic book or will it be in a cinematic or electronic incarnation? On a more intimate scale, will it touch a child or adult and motivate him or her to think or to act?

Perhaps it is foolhardy even to think such things as one creates, since it is more realistic and saner to focus on the deadline and the paycheck. But the creative act, even when most cynically pursued, is still an (unconscious) stab at immortality. Who wouldn't want to create the next Superman, the next Wonder Woman, the next Spider-Man?

Which leads us to wonder . . . what did the creators of Superman think they were creating? The next Samson perhaps? Or the next Doc Savage? Did they realize they had created something never exactly before seen?

Which then leads us to ask: Is a superhero a superhero outside the confines of a comic book?

There are two answers to this, one obvious, the other less so.

Answer 1: Of course. Batman in the comics and Batman in the movies and Batman in a cartoon series are the same basic character, the same representation of an aspect of the human condition. Batman is a dark avenger of the night, traumatized by violent childhood loss into an obsessed hunter of criminals, avenging his parents' murder again and again with his defeat of every criminal he pursues. His lack of ability to achieve closure around the issues of loss and revenge is his personal neurosis, but it is the gain of the city and society in which he operates. That's Batman, no matter where he appears. The emphasis on whatever aspect —camp, as in the 1960s TV series; noir-inflected drama, as in the 1990s animated series; future techno-drama, as in the Batman Beyond series—is more a function of the times and the creative team behind a particular incarnation. But the basic mythos is always the same.

But what of superheroic characters whose origins are in other media? Are they superheroes? This brings us to answer 2.

Buffy the Vampire Slayer is surely a superhero (or superheroine, if you like). To be more specific, she occupies the subgenre of "horror superhero comics." That is to say, she generally does not pursue muggers, bank robbers, terrorists, or even common murderers. Her "beat"—made less coincidental by her living near the "Hellmouth" nexus of evil—is demons, monsters, and, of course, vampires. Buffy has superhuman strength and agility, enhanced senses, and a sense of duty and destiny. She has a support group composed of nonenhanced aides, as well as masters and mistresses of magical arts, and "reformed" vampires, the latter of which she regularly becomes romantically involved with. Seems like all the ingredients for superhero drama there. And Joss Whedon, the character's creator, makes no secret of his love for and influence by superhero comics. Buffy even appears in a regular series of comics and graphic novels.

One could argue that Buffy is a TV character, despite her origins in a feature-length movie. But that is a fairly flimsy argument. And, given the continual and historical exploitation of superpowered characters across a variety of media—today very few such characters are created without the pitch somewhere mentioning such possibilities—the boundaries are more blurred than ever. And, as I will show, the continued cross-pollination between incarnations of superheroes from one medium to another has been part of the entertainment megaculture since there was more than one mass medium that a character could appear in.

Indeed, given the shift in the contemporary audience for comics, one could ask a child if he or she likes Spider-Man.

"Sure," our hypothetical youngster would answer. "I love Spider-Man. I've seen the movie five times. I own the DVD. I play all the Spidey video games."

But were one to ask this child: "When was the last time you bought a Spider-Man comic?" the answer would most likely be, "What's a comic?"

Still, you would most definitely call such a child a fan of superheroes—or at least of one superhero, Spider-Man, in this case.

The challenge in answering the question is less in defining clearly superhuman characters such as Buffy or Angel. They have powers "above and beyond those of mortal men" (or women). They fight for good against evil, often in cases where the evil is considerate enough to identify itself as such, in deed if not in word.

The challenging and interesting cases where the definitions are harder to come by are in situations where the challenges to, and worldviews of, characters edge over into superhero territory, but the other markers of superhero fiction may not be there.

Is Clint Eastwood's Dirty Harry a superhero? If he wore a mask and cape, would he be a more violent version of Batman? After all, Harry never seems to kill the wrong people, he takes more punishment than any ten men could, and he always has a clear sense of right and wrong. In one of the Dirty Harry films, the point of the story is to show that even Harry—a rough-and-ready cop with a really big gun—is still on the side of the angels compared to a cabal of vigilante cops, a splinter shadow group within the department. Harry breaks the rules all right—but knows just how many can be broken and still maintain an open society. At least that's the fantasy.

What about Rambo? What about the heroes of the *Lethal Weapon* movies? What about Charlie's Angels? These characters all live in worlds where magic has no hold and where the rules of physics are generally held to be in force. And for most people in these works, that is true. But isn't it a kind of magic that Sylvester Stallone, Danny Glover, and Mel Gibson are never killed or permanently disabled by the physical abuse and sheer quantity of flying bullets they seem to perpetually attract? If not magic, one would think they have their own personally generated force fields, no doubt a function of some sort of mininuclear reactors they must have strapped to their backs. But no such assertion is made. Clearly, these characters are in some kind of middle world between fictional superheroes and human heroes.

So is James Bond. Bond—from the very beginning of his film career (the original Ian Fleming books, the early ones at any rate, were written in a more realistic vein)—has always gone pretty easily over the edge into superhumanness. From the moment he received his arsenal-disguised-as-an attaché case in *From Russia with Love*, it was clear his world was not exactly ours. Or perhaps the moment when Dr. No appeared in his spaceman-like garb, complete with enhanced artificial hands, was the moment when we knew that the cinematic Bond was bound to be some kind of superhero.

What I think unites these different heroic characters is what I call "superhero comic consciousness," by which I mean the hope (and fear) that there may be more to this world than what we see. Why is it important to us to plant such a possibility in our popular cultural diet? That may really be the true topic of this book. Why do we need that element of fantasy in our heroes, even many of the so-called realistic ones? What need do these fantasies fulfill? What societal function is served by our sitting around our virtual print, cinematic, or electronic campfires to tell and hear the stories of these people who, in essence, make it safe for us to get up and go about our daily activities? And why, inevitably, do their adversaries and exploits take on a bigger-than-life quality? Then again, perhaps in a world that creates a Hitler, a Stalin, a Pol Pot, the need to create a pantheon of righteous super-powered saviors, who are not anybody's deities, is an understandable and inevitable response.

Or, to put it more simply, is the superhero in us—or are we in the superhero?

Up, up—and *away!*

2

It Started With Gilgamesh
The History of the Superhero

Commercial fiction panders to low tastes and traffics in scandal, violence and sentimentality; the art novel appeals to cultivated tastes and traffics in the same commodities, but in a more genteel way.

Thomas M. Disch, *The Dreams Our Stuff Is Made Of*

TRACING the history of the superhero proves no less daunting —and no less interesting—than defining what, exactly, a superhero is.

Again, as long as there have been humans gathered around a campfire or a screen, people have wanted to hear tales of heroism. And as long as there has been the desire to hear such stories, there has been the need to hear tales of beings whose powers and abilities—indeed, whose joys and sorrows, gains and losses—are greater than those that we know and encounter in our daily lives. Why would people need to hear such exaggerated stories? Aren't tales of true human valor enough? If fiction is needed, wouldn't ordinary-seeming, or even extraordinary people, facing extraordinary circumstances best serve as role models and inspirations? Wouldn't the very thought of superhuman beings make us all feel pitifully inadequate? Or is it easier to read of a superior being from beyond the stars outclassing us than of a guy from down the block who was just luckier or stronger or smarter?

Maybe that's the key. Maybe we feel uncomfortable with the idea that we're not living up to our potential, or that someone else has more potential than we do. Or that they're living up to their potential better than we are to ours?

But if that someone else isn't really playing on the same field or by the same rules we do . . . then maybe we don't have to feel so bad about ourselves. I suppose this would characterize the Superman fan more than, say, the Batman fan.

Superman is from Krypton. We can't be from Krypton. No need to feel any worse about not being him than one would about not being able to stop a hurricane. But Batman . . . he was a normal seven-year old who, over his parents' murdered corpses swore a vow to be better, stronger, smarter—or to use his intelligence to its limits—than anyone else. Not only did he swear that—he did it! So maybe he makes you a little uncomfortable. Maybe you couldn't even keep that New Year's resolution to lose ten pounds.

Of course, Batman, too, is bigger than life and displays superhuman characteristics. In this he is similar to the Lone Ranger, as described by John Shelton Lawrence and Robert Jewett in *The Myth of the American Superhero.*

> . . . the Lone Ranger never kills anyone. With superhuman accuracy, his silver bullets strike the hands of threatening bad guys—evoking a mere "yow!" or "my hand!" Yet their evil powers are neutralized . . . the Lone Ranger's powers ensure that he inflicts minimal injury.—40

Even the "real world" heroes of our popular culture seem to operate on planes where various kinds of magic are at work. Could the heroes portrayed by John Wayne or Sylvester Stallone really dodge as many bullets as they do if they were real? Could the Punisher or Dirty Harry really fire as many times as they do and not incur significant quantities of collateral damage? Of course not. And yet, these heroes are considered "normal."

For most of us, if we were ever in a fistfight, if we ever were socked in, or socked anybody else in the jaw, it would be a remarkable event. We would tell the story to our friends over and over. We'd pass it down to our children. We'd go to various specialists to make sure we weren't permanently hurt, and make it our business to have arrested and to sue whomever it was who did hit us. It would be a major event.

Yet, to even the most "human" of serial fiction heroes, physical conflict is a regular, part-of-the-job, virtually daily occurrence. Has there ever been an episode of *Gunsmoke* when Marshal Dillon has not engaged in at least one fistfight? And in the case of drawn characters who need not depend on the flesh and blood presence of a particular actor, the number of battles is simply staggering. In the course of sixty-plus years, just how many hand-to-hand fights has Batman been in? How many battles has superspy Nick Fury been party to? The number, if not literally countless, is certainly beyond the action quotient of even the most grizzled, testosterone-fueled, real-world combatant.

So the fact must be that, even in their "real" heroes, people need to see powers and abilities far beyond those that the rest of us—even the best of us—are capable of displaying. And in such a case, it stands to reason that, from the adventures of a "regular" guy acting at "peak human" ability (as the official character catalog, the *Marvel Universe Handbook,* refers to it), we would then move into the tall tales of characters such as John Henry, Paul Bunyon, and Buffalo Bill. From there, it's a matter of incremental leaps to the next levels.

A significant point is related to that sock in the jaw mentioned above. For all but professional street brawlers and gang members, that punch would be a life-changing event. Indeed, any event that rises above—or below—the everyday is an event that will change people's attitudes, bodies, minds, relationships. Life is about change, be it incremental or tidal. As you sit reading this, changes are going on inside and around you. The sun moving across the sky, the changes in the level of the ocean, the growth of hair are less noticeable than a sudden car crash might be. But change is constant. The policeman on the beat may be involved in a shootout that will injure himself or others, or he may just work his twenty and retire to a quiet fishing boat.

But Superman will not retire. He, too, will change—a Superman comic or movie of today looks significantly different from one of the 1940s. But he will be the Superman for that era, in principle the same individual who came to Earth from Krypton however many years ago.

Like the gods of various pantheons, the superheroes do not change.

Comics writers refer to their characters being allowed the "illusion of change." This is true of all serial characters, and may, strangely, be part of their appeal. We grow older, our friends and relatives grow older—even die, eventually—but the superheroes are always there. If they age at all, it's extraordinarily slowly. We learn and grow—we *change*—from experience. For the most part, serialized fictional characters do not. This is at once a great strength and a terrific weakness for them.

A great story can be defined as a story in which characters come into conflict—physical or psychic—and through dealing with that conflict grow and change. Ishmael is a different character at the conclusion of *Moby-Dick* from what he was at the beginning. Tom Joad is a different character at the beginning of *The Grapes of Wrath* from what he is at its ending. These characters are allowed to change. Indeed, the pleasure of reading is watching as they change, experiencing life-altering events with them.

In life, how we change as we age, how we, it is hoped, learn from our experiences and acquire some measure of wisdom, is one of the inevitable consequences of being alive. Watching others go through the same thing can be inspirational and instructive. We learn and grow and change. And we hope these changes will be for the better somehow. There is no avoiding change.

But for superheroes, change is tremendously slow, and more often, nonexistent. Superman may have to keep his secret identity from Lana Lang in the *Smallville* TV series and other incarnations of the young Clark Kent, but we all know that, as he grows up, he will be keeping his secret from Lois Lane.

Now, you may say, in current comics continuity, Lois and Clark are a happily married couple, as are Spider-Man and Mary Jane Watson. Are these situations "change" or merely the illusion of such? They could be classified as actual changes, but they are the *exception* rather than the rule. Certainly, Spider-Man's identity is still secret, he still fights a recurring roster of villains, with the occasional new one thrown in.

Perhaps as significantly, Spider-Man exists in a secondary line—Marvel's *Ultimate* line—in which he is an unmarried teenager and Mary Jane is his girlfriend. And, certainly, the incarnation of the character most people currently know—the Tobey Maguire Spider-Man of the movie screen—is the unattached, troubled teenager. Superman—single, of course—in current movies and cartoons still plays the same cat-and-mouse vis-à-vis his secret identity with the hot-and-cold running Lois. The audience for these versions is vastly larger than that of the comics, whose readers can perhaps take a little pseudorealism in their stories (If characters who fight mutants and regularly communicate telepathically can be said to be realistic.)

But whatever the version, married or single, perpetual adolescent or slowly maturing young adult, the no-change rule still holds quite firmly. Even the married Spider-Man and Superman have not aged more than what seems like a few months since their marriages over a decade ago. Certainly they have remained childless. That they are married just means the artists and writers who create their stories are now denied the convenient plot devices of romantic drama with its rivalries and uncertainties. The gain? Well, in theory, shutting up the "nothing can really change" critics, and, if the comics audience is aging, then a married, settled down superhero could be thought to be easier to relate to. Unless, of course, the reader's intent in reading is to indulge in a fantasy about being young and unencumbered by adult commitments.

Can a character who doesn't age ever learn and change? Only in the most superficial ways. He or she cannot truly change, since change involves various kinds of closure and transition. Maybe Batman would have a need to be Batman, a need that would diminish and eventually fade away after a couple of years in real life. Perhaps he would sustain an injury that would disable him. Perhaps he would accidentally hurt an innocent person. Perhaps he would be arrested himself for vigilante violence. Some of these things have happened to him in various story lines, but the final consequence can never be the character deciding he's had enough, it's too tough, or even that he was wrong to set out on his mission in the first place. Too many real people's dreams . . . too many real people's *incomes* . . . depend on the heroes staying evergreen.

And we're thankful for this. Just as we're thankful for Hester Prynne and Oliver Twist, and the other icons of fiction. We're always disappointed at the conclusion of a great book that our relationship with these characters is over. With serial fiction, the relationships never have to end. The connections we feel can be repeated indefinitely. What we lose in the process are some of the highs and lows of dramatic experience. We know that Superman won't die—even when a major marketing campaign proclaims SUPERMAN DIES! There's a permanence there, a continuity, a sense of predictability that means a lot to us in a world as uncertain as ours is—and as uncertain, surely, as the world has always been. Even the most peaceful, stable place is not immune from aging, decay, and death.

But the world of superheroes is. And that may be their greatest power and the one that ultimately means the most to us. Although our lives are fragile and subject to countless unpredictable phenomena, the lives of the costumed adventurers will transcend that of any actor or writer or artist—or audience member.

We achieve immortality through the superheroes.

Why and how did the specific iconic characters we think of as "The Superheroes" come to be the ones we know and love, not merely personally but on a collective, societal basis?

After all, there have been heroic myths for as long as there has been human communication and storytelling. From the Bible stories of Samson and Moses, even the origins and eventual fate of Jesus have many of the trappings of heroic fiction.

Shakespeare's plays are certainly a spring from which many a modern yarn has been spun. Hamlet and Lear are certainly inspiration for Marvel Comics' Thor and Odin characters. Falstaff becomes Volstagg in that mythology. And would there be a Dr. Doom—or a Darth Vader, for that matter—without the transcendent villainy of Shakespeare's Richard III?

Gilgamesh's battles against mortality itself, Beowulf's confrontations with Grendel and the monsters, all resonate with what would later become the stuff of superhero legends.

Yet there are no schoolyard arguments over who's stronger—Gilgamesh or Moses? No Internet flame wars over whether Shiva could kick Delilah's rear. Maybe it would seem sacrilegious to do so.

Joseph Campbell's *The Hero with a Thousand Faces* relates the Mono-myth of which all heroic fiction is comprised. Christopher Vogler codi-fies these theses for the modern screenwriter. C. G. Jung writes about "the universal hero." These works all tell us why the heroic myth—and specifically, stories of people with superhuman qualities—has rever-berated for millennia with humans. But there is no Gilgamesh movie drawing crowds at the multiplex.

Yet the works these scholars write of are mostly relegated to the realm of academic scholarship and esoteric journals. The myths they discuss may have become embedded in world consciousness, but the specific characters are as foreign to most of us as hieroglyphs on a pyra-mid wall.

Edgar Allan Poe, Jules Verne, and Arthur Conan Doyle could be seen as the progenitors—the "real writers"—behind the explosion of what would come to be called the pulps. According to Jim Steranko in *The Steranko History of Comics,* vol. 1: "Pulps were untrimmed maga-zines, named for the soft paper flecked with shreds of wood fiber on which they were printed. Publishers used pulp paper because there was nothing cheaper available."

Steranko continues: "Pulps measured 9½" × 7½" and had 114 to 162 pages between full color enamel stock covers. Most had 128 pages, which usually featured a lead novel of some 50,000 to 60,000 words and a half dozen short stories totaling an additional 20,000 words. Some books featured more stories of shorter length, again totaling about 80,000 words."

In other words, literally millions of words, comprising thousands of stories were published on a regular basis, many of them featuring action adventure tales in the Western, mystery, science fiction, and jungle adventure genres, all featuring bigger-than-life heroes and heroines. The appetite for such stories was there. But there were still no characters one could call superheroes.

In the 1920s and 1930s, there was a kind of synergistic back-and-forth between the troika of pulps, movies, and radio. Characters like the Shadow—who starred in an astonishing number of pulp novels (also known as dime novels)—started in rough form in one medium, were modified in another, and then, with those changes intact, would become thus modified in his "original" form. Like a game of cross-media telephone, the characters evolved in the manner that folk heroes always had, but through modern communications technology, the various incarnations were transmitted simultaneously to thousands and millions of eager readers, viewers and listeners.

As Reynolds notes in *Super Heroes: A Modern Mythology:*

> *Avenging 'Lone Wolf' heroes abounded in popular narrative of the 1930s and '40s on both sides of the Atlantic: from Doc Savage to Philip Marlowe, from Hannay in Hitchcock's* 39 Steps *to the Green Hornet, from Rick Blaine in* Casablanca *to Captain Midnight of the radio serials. A new kind of popular hero had emerged: the self-reliant individualist who stands aloof from many of the humdrum concerns of society, yet is able to operate according to his own code of honor, to take on the world on his own terms and win.—18*

Certainly, in a nation where literacy was growing at an enormous rate, as was the ability to mass-produce literature, or something resembling literature, the audience for such excitement-generating page-turners was set to grow indefinitely. In their lifetimes, Hawthorne and Melville never had numbers like the pulp writers would—and on a monthly basis yet! The thirst for heroic adventure was insatiable. Prolific pulp writers typed, literally, until their fingers bled.

The Shadow set the pace. He was the ultimate supernaturally tinged avenger of evil. Although he was not literally masked, his true identities—several of them—were unknown to any but his closest associates.

The next ingredient in the creation of the superhero was the addition, of course, of power beyond that of any human. This was seen early on in the person of Doc Savage, the Man of Bronze, a popular pulp hero who was a big influence on Superman co-creator Jerry Siegel. Steranko notes: "Walter Baumhofer, Doc's first and foremost cover artist, was requested to make the Man of Bronze resemble Clark Gable as much as possible." Again, the influence of movies on the creation of a popular fictional character who would in part inspire another, to-be-more-famous character is seen.

"The source for the essence of Superman and his development," continues Steranko, "was influenced by Philip Wylie's striking novel, *Gladiator*. Published in 1930, it served as a blueprint for Siegel's character,"

> *Siegel's Superman concept embodied and amalgamated three separate and distinct themes: the visitor from another planet; the superhuman being, and the dual identity. He composed the Superman charisma by exploiting all three elements, and all three contributed equally to the eventual success of the strip. His inspiration, of course, came from the science fiction pulps.—37*

It would be impossible to discuss the pulps without mentioning their most popular—and earliest genre—the Western. And the grandfather of all Western characters was Buffalo Bill Cody. Though a real, historical figure, Cody's chronicled life took on the elements of the wildest fictional characters. According to Lawrence and Jewett in *The Myth of the American Superhero:*

> *The decisive formation of western heroic imagery took place when the daring and attractive William F. Cody began to style himself as "Buffalo Bill." Showman Cody convincingly played the redeemer role for the Wild West*

show audiences. . . . In the self-portraits of the shows and the seventeen hundred novels and stories written about his exploits—many written with his collaboration—Cody developed this heroic image with brazen exaggerations that even he privately acknowledged were unrealistic.—50

It was Cody who took the gritty, bloody reality of the expansion of the American West and made of it the spectacle of touring shows that re-enacted his greatest triumphs. Even while still living the life of the frontier adventurer, Cody was reenacting his greatest battles in elaborate traveling spectacular shows.

John Burke, one of Cody's biographers, comments on this:

Would Achilles, for instance, have abandoned the forces laying siege to Troy and hurried back to Athens to play himself before a crowded amphitheater? No matter, this was modern America, where a man had the right to cash in on his fame.

—John Burke, *Buffalo Bill, the Noblest Whiteskin* (as quoted in Lawrence and Jewett's *Myth of the American Superhero*)—95

Cody's adventures were transferred from whatever was their basis in reality into prose fiction beginning with the efforts of Ned Buntline. His 1869 *Buffalo Bill: The King of the Border Men* actually combined and exaggerated the exploits of Cody and Wild Bill Hickock into something well beyond any real representation of either. A nation coming to grips with the savagery of its own expansionism needed myths and heroes it could believe in. Buntline and others gave them those myths.

The tales of Buffalo Bill inspired the hundreds of dime novels that followed, with adventure-filled tales of Cody and of many lesser lights of the West, real, fictional, and the combination of the two.

The archetypal 1902 Western novel *The Virginian*, by Owen Wister, was important in solidifying the Western myth, with its depiction of the first "showdown" in American literature. The villain, of course, draws first, but is killed by the hero, whose aim—and heart—is truer.

It was these Western legends that culminated in the adventures of the masked Lone Ranger. In many ways, the Ranger prefigures the masked superheroes of the comics. Created in 1933 by writers at a Detroit radio station, the Ranger's origin echoes that of many of the masked adventurers who would come to populate the superhero mythos. Along with Zorro, who would be one of the inspirations that led Bob Kane to create Batman, the Ranger focused various myths and added his own elements such as the silver bullets (especially effective, in pop culture, against vampires) and the sidekick. These were all some ingredients that would be added to the cultural stew from which the superhero would emerge.

Backtracking in time a bit, it was in 1896 that the two most important elements in the formation of the superhero mythos were created,

Richard F. Outcault's "The Yellow Kid," generally regarded as the first modern newspaper comic strip, made its debut in William Randolph Hearst's *New York Journal*. The Kid inaugurated the onslaught of comic-strip characters that would become America's most popular pre-radio, pre-television entertainment. Krazy Kat, The Katzenjammer Kids, Popeye, and dozens of other characters emerged from the newspaper strips. The strips were what sold newspapers.

Also in that year, publisher Frank Munsey released what is regarded as the first pulp magazine, *The Argosy*. As Les Daniels notes in his *Marvel: Five Fabulous Decades of the World's Greatest Comics*: "With this innovation—undertaken, as noted, because it was the cheapest paper available—he also switched from children's stories to tales of action and adventure, emphasizing a type of fast-moving fiction that is still called 'pulp' today."

Munsey's top writer was Edgar Rice Burroughs, whose creations—most notably, in 1912, of Tarzan of the Apes—became the models on which future pulp heroes would be based.

Black Mask magazine was the pulp that introduced the hard-boiled private eye to popular culture, in stories written by Dashiell Hammett and Raymond Chandler, among others.

Amazing Stories began the science-fiction craze, and would be the birthplace of Philip Nowlan's Buck Rogers.

Weird Tales would showcase the talents of H. P. Lovecraft, Ray Bradbury, and was the birthplace of Robert E. Howard's Conan.

At last, in 1929, the two media—newspaper strips and pulp magazines—that had been fermenting separately, finally came together. Tarzan was translated into a newspaper strip by Hal Foster. The same year, Dick Calkins would translate Nowlan's Buck Rogers into strip form. The adventure comic strip was born. It was an invention that would shape much of popular heroic fiction as we know it today.

Soon, according to Daniels:

> . . . Crime fighting moved into the funny pages with Chester Gould's grim detective "Dick Tracy" in 1931, and pulp writer Dashiell Hammett got into the act in 1934 with "Secret Agent X-9," illustrated by Alex Raymond. In the same year, Raymond introduced his spectacular science fiction strip "Flash Gordon." Lee Falk and Ray Moore's "The Phantom" had a mask and a secret identity, and was the first comics character to dress in tights from head to toe.—16

Martin Goodman was one of the major pulp publishers. With magazines like *Marvel Science Stories*, he produced a high volume of popular, if not highly original, publications. Occasional continuing characters such as Ka-Zar (a Tarzan type jungle character) would appear in his magazines, but generally Goodman published—under a plethora of corporate names—in his Red Circle line of pulps, stand-alone stories of action and adventure.

Meanwhile, publishers had been collecting newspaper strips of various types and reprinting them in "comic books." These books were composed of large sheets of newsprint, folded and trimmed into magazine shape. When the old material ran out, new material was commissioned, including the first *themed* comic book, National's *Detective Comics*.

In 1938, Superman debuted in National Periodicals's *Action Comics* #1, and the character was an immediate hit. He was followed up in 1939, in *Detective Comics* number 27, with Batman, who proved nearly as popular.

Although comics didn't kill the pulps, which would be printed until the 1950s, they began, according to Daniels, "to outsell the pulps almost at once. . . . Publishers like Goodman, who were successful with the new form because of their background in distribution, tended to lose interest in the pulps, especially when wartime paper rationing forced them to make a choice" (page 23).

Again, the symbiotic pop-culture cycle would continue, as comics heroes spawned radio programs, movies (features and serials), whereas movies continued to inspire and energize comics writers and artists.

To greater or lesser degrees, this process continued down through the decades. In every decade, at least, there has been some superhero icon. The 1950s had the popular *Superman* TV series. The 1960s saw the campy but no-less-popular *Batman* show. The 1970s had Bill Bixby and Lou Ferrigno in *The Incredible Hulk;* the 1980s and 1990s *Batman* movies; and the current decade has the spate of Marvel Comics-based movies such as *X-Men, Spider-Man,* and *Blade*. The need to deal metaphorically with our dreams and hopes, our fears and anxieties through the short-hand of the superhero remains as universal as ever.

Of course, different people know of these cultural icons from different media. Some know them from movies, some from television, some from the comics themselves, and, indeed, many may just know that the characters exist but not know exactly how or from where they know about them. The superhero has evolved in our collective consciousness to the point where it may not even matter where the concept originally came from.

So we can say that the pulps, the comic strips, and the movies of the 1930s were rivers fed by thousands of years of storytelling about heroes. These rivers flowed into the ocean of consciousness that birthed the comic book superhero, an entity that would grow and develop into a concept that, today, is one of the few universal fictional concepts known the world over.

Now, let's adjust the microscope, and see in more detail just what aspects of our society are reflected by the various heroes.

3

The Dual Identity

Of Pimpernels and Immigrants
from the Stars

Though a disguise, Kent is necessary for the [Superman] myth to work. This uniquely American hero has two identities, one based on where he comes from in life's journey, one on where he's going. One is real, one an illusion, and both are necessary for the myth of balance in the assimilation process to be complete. Superman's powers make the hero capable of saving humanity; Kent's total immersion in the American heartland makes him want to do it. The result is . . . an optimistic myth of assimilation . . .

> Gary Engle, "What Makes Superman So Darned American?," in *Superman at Fifty: The Persistence of a Legend,* edited by Dennis Dooley and Gary Engle

We are what we pretend to be, so we must be careful about what we pretend to be.

> Kurt Vonnegut, *Mother Night*

WHY does a person disguise his or her identity? There can be myriad reasons, although the very act can seem counterintuitive. Most people want *credit* for acts they are proud of. That is the nature of pride: "I made this," as the child's voice—the real or imagined voice of creator Chris Carter—says at the end of every episode of *The X-Files*.

In real life, there are many reasons people have for habitually disguising their identities or their actions. The most obvious would be the criminal who wears a mask so he will not be identified for future pursuit and incarceration.

The same can be said for acts of political or social courage in societies where such activities would be punished severely. Think of the masked mob informant or the hooded dissident in the Middle East. Or think of the Ku Klux Klan and its hooded cross burners. Their friends certainly know who they are, but their hoods keep them from being identified by their victims and by law-enforcement organizations. Plus, a mask or hood injects an element of terror into an individual's presence and presentation. The sight of many such hooded individuals massed together is the stuff of nightmares.

There are anonymous philanthropists who modestly wish that their acts speak for themselves, not for their own personal glorification.

There are graffiti artists whose "tags" consistently identify that they were there, but not who they are when you pass them on the street.

There is the anonymity of the telephone and the Internet, and of radio call-in shows, where the cloak of mystery gives people the courage to do and say things—either socially accepted as "good" or "bad," "right" or "wrong"—without fear of repercussion. Again, depending on the context and the intent, the hidden identity can be used to positive or negative effect. What is the popular *Crank Yankers* TV series but the exploits of anonymous phone pranksters, individuals usually seen as at best annoying and at worst criminally harassing? Generally, no one is permanently harmed by a phone prankster. Still, you'd be hard pressed to admire one, even one you found amusing.

How then, does this idea of disguise fit into our popular culture, and why has it become a staple, indeed one of the very definitions of, the superhero mythos?

In his classic routine "Thank You, Masked Man" (also made into an animated short), Lenny Bruce commented on the cliché of the masked hero—in this case the Lone Ranger—not only keeping his identity secret, but not even waiting around to be thanked. The reason for both these cultural conventions, according to Bruce—himself the "secret identity" of Leonard Schneider—is that the masked man doesn't want to get used to being thanked. If he became too dependent on it, how would he feel if he ever wasn't thanked? He wants to keep his motive pure: to make sure he does what he does because it's right, not to get thanked. So that may be a piece of why masked heroes appeal to us. They want their deeds to stand alone. That's a valid human desire that we can sympathize with.

Where did dual identity stories begin? Was it when Jacob disguised himself as Esau to get his father's blessing? Or was it Odysseus disguising himself in the pages of *The Odyssey*? Was it in the story where Leah disguised herself so that Jacob would marry her and not her sister? Going to Shakespeare, where would he have been without the disguises and impersonations used in *Twelfth Night* and *A Midsummer Night's Dream*? Disguise and deception have a long and honorable tradition in fiction, if not in real life.

To take us into the realm of heroic and superheroic disguises, we would probably start with Baroness Orczy's *Scarlet Pimpernel* mythology. Published in 1905, the *Pimpernel* tells of the adventures of Sir Percy Blanckney, a fop and layabout who, it turns out, is also a master of disguise. As portrayed in the 1935 movie, starring Leslie Howard, the Pimpernel's alter ego is that of the most shallow and vain, albeit charming and witty, type of English aristocrat. But his secret agenda is to rescue *French* aristocrats who are condemned en masse to death at the guillotine by Robespierre and the excesses of the French Revolution.

The Pimpernel is not so much a mask as an attitude and a series of disguises. When at last discovered by his French nemesis—and his own wife, from whom he conceals his secret life—the Pimpernel still looks the same physically, but his carriage is suddenly more serious and dangerous. You can see this device used to comic effect by Jerry Lewis in *The Nutty Professor*, or, indeed, by Superman himself when he puts on the glasses that allegedly fool the world into thinking he and Clark Kent are two different people. Even the genre of teen movies in which a "plain" girl becomes glamorous always involves her removing glasses (and undoing her hair) to show the "secret identity" of the sexpot within.

What fantasy does the double identity appeal to? Perhaps, as in the case of the Pimpernel, it is to allow us to believe that, deep down, we are or could be so much more than we appear. "If they only knew how special I am," we think. Don't we all have secret identities, those sides of ourselves we feel we dare not risk revealing? The secret identity is where our fantasies and ambitions take hold and ferment. We eagerly seek the time when we can give free reign to the "superhero within." But there is risk in being one's true self. Indeed, what if people don't like the real you? Well then, you can always go back, at least temporarily, to the pretend-you that they did like. Of course, in our real lives, there's much overlap between the "real" and the façade. One is always seeping into and through the other. A mask, a dual identity, makes the demarcation so much easier for us as well as those to whom we want to project our identities.

When you think of a mask, your first thought is of a criminal. This writer still recalls with a shiver the bandanna-wearing "Western Bandits" who demanded "all your gold," at an amusement park when he was a child. A mask is scary. It reduces the person wearing it to a single, sinister element. They are a living threat. You cannot reason with them. Their expression betrays no meaning beyond what their words say. They cannot be up to any good—nor mean you anything but harm. If they did, why would they cover their faces—or at least their true identities—and eschew responsibility for their actions?

So how did the masked hero come to be? (And here, I use the term *masked* as the superheroes do, both literally and metaphorically. A physical mask is not necessary to conceal identity, at least not among the superheroes.)

Through time and across civilizations, the mask has had much power and magic associated with it. African and South American shamans and priests wore ceremonial garb to perform their rituals, often with a mask as part of their costume. Clearly, the mask in such cases is not intended to fool anyone as to the identity of the wearer. It is simultaneously intended to make the wearer special and nondescript, the Everyman raised to the level of interlocutor with the holy. The mask is recognized as bestower of power as well as disguiser of identity.

A mask is intimidating. So why *should* it be confined to use by criminals? Why not use that intimidation factor against those who would do individuals or society harm on whatever scale? In real life, this leads to the aforementioned Ku Klux Klan and other vigilante and terrorist organizations. In the world of heroic fiction, though, such an affectation can be used to turn the tables on those who would do harm.

In the modern era, Zorro may be thought of as the first masked adventurer. Created by Johnston McCulley in his novel *The Curse of Capistrano*, which began its serialization in the August 9, 1919, issue of *All-Story Weekly* (the same magazine that introduced Tarzan), Zorro was the archetypal indolent rich laggard whose laziness and ennui were a cover for a passionate fighter for freedom. In such a case, Zorro needed a secret identity so that he could continue his life as an insider in the halls of power and wealth, privy to the goings on of the rich and powerful whom he could protect from those who would plunder their wealth, and whose rotten apples he could ferret out untroubled. Zorro, especially his movie incarnation in *The Mark of Zorro* in 1920, was certainly one of the role models for later masked heroes.

The Phantom, by Lee Falk and Ray Moore, was the first masked hero in the comic strips, and the first hero to adopt the trunks and leotard outfit—a legacy from circus performers of the time—and combine it with a cowl and a black mask that revealed no visible eyeballs. The Phantom's reason for the mask was to create the illusion of immortality, as one Phantom after another passed the mantle to a son.

Then there is the classic reason heroes give for maintaining dual identities: it will protect my loved ones from my enemies. That has some credence, until you stop to think about it. Does the policeman on the neighborhood beat have a secret identity? Does the teacher who works with delinquent kids? Come to think of it—maybe they should. Except, for the fact that that sort of thinking is where phenomena such as death squads emerge. Masked justice is rarely blind justice. Masked justice has an agenda, and in real life, the agenda is rarely to just give the police an extra "edge."

Spies may be seen as a subset of the dual-identity character. Even the flamboyant James Bond is, technically, an undercover operative. Often, in real life, spies are who they say they are, though their agendas are not what they purport them to be. And spies, even ones on "our side," are generally thought of as sneaky and untrustworthy. We accept that they have to be to do a dirty job on our behalf. But when espionage is presented outside the worlds of the *Alias* TV series and James Bond, it does indeed seem . . . well, underhanded. The CIA agents of the recent series *The Agency* are not really very nice people. Part of the reason for this is, well, they're always lying about who they really are.

Only the superhero disguises his identity for a noble purpose and is able to maintain his integrity while so doing. Why?

The secret identity, as Gary Engle notes, is deeply rooted in the American immigrant experience. As the *Ur* superhero, Superman is also the easiest and most direct manifestation of the dual identity. As Engle points out in his essay "What Makes Superman So Darned American?":

> *The brilliant stroke in the conception of Superman—the* sine qua non *that makes the whole myth work—is the fact that he has two identities. The myth simply wouldn't work without Clark Kent, mild-mannered newspaper reporter . . . Adopting the white-bread image of a wimp is first and foremost a moral act for the Man of Steel. He does it to protect his parents from nefarious sorts who might use them to gain an edge over the powerful alien. Moreover, Kent adds to Superman's powers the moral guidance of a Smallville upbringing. Clark Kent . . . is the epitome of visible invisibility, someone whose extraordinary ordinariness makes him disappear in a crowd. In a phrase, he is the consummate figure of total cultural assimilation, and significantly, he is not real. Implicit in this is the notion that mainstream cultural norms, however useful, are illusions.*

So, according to Engle, the immigrant origin is at the heart of the Superman dual identity. It's just that Superman is from another planet instead of another country. Superman's story is not unlike that of the kid who at home speaks the language of his parents' immigrant roots, but outside adopts the identity of the mainstream, attempting to blend in and become one with the adopted homeland. But the "regular guy" is the sham persona—because the power underneath is just too dangerous for people to be allowed to observe it any time they desire. The immigrant wants to excel but stay anonymous. He wants to make his parents proud—but not make them ashamed of who they themselves are, though he may, himself, be ashamed of them in certain profound ways.

In Siegel and Shuster's case, the home was the Yiddish-speaking, or at least Yiddish-inflected, home of the Eastern European Jewish immigrant stock they came from. The duo struggled with many of the same issues Superman did. Immigration and assimilation were issues that even a space-born superbeing could not avoid. As Engle notes:

Immigration, of course, is the overwhelming fact in American history. Except for the Indians, all Americans have an immediate sense of their origins elsewhere. No nation on Earth has so deeply embedded in its social consciousness the imagery of passage from one social identity to another. . . .—80

further,

*Superman's powers . . . are the comic book equivalents of ethnic characteristics, and they protect and preserve the vitality of the foster community in which he lives in the same way that immigrant ethnicity has sustained American culture linguistically, artistically, economically, politically and spiritually. **The myth of Superman asserts with total confidence and a childlike innocence the value of the immigrant in American culture.** [Emphasis mine.]—81*

and,

Clinging to an Old World identity meant isolation in ghettos, confrontation with a prejudiced mainstream culture, second-class social status and impoverishment. On the other hand, forsaking the past in favor of total absorption into the mainstream, while it could result in socio-economic progress, meant a loss of the religious, linguistic, even culinary traditions that provided a foundation for psychological well-being.—83

For the readers of early superhero stories, many of whom were children and grandchildren of immigrants, the characters were a symbolic reenactment of their own ambivalent feelings about where their roots lay, and where their lives in America were taking them. Dual identity superheroes would enable these readers to inhabit both sides of their dilemma. "Am I who I am at home, or am I the person I am outside my home? Which is the real me? Which is true and which false? Who should I *want* to be?"

In many ways, don't we all feel like strangers in a strange land when we first venture outside our homes to school or to work? Love home or hate it, it is familiar. We know who we must be to survive and possibly thrive there. But who do we become when we have some choice in what faces we present to the world? These are hard and basic choices we all have to make from our earliest days, certainly at first without even being aware that we're making them.

The superheroes make these choices in grander, more melodramatic, more colorful levels. But they clearly echo our own choices as we venture from the familiar terrain of home out into the world.

But Superman isn't merely an immigrant. He is an immigrant *orphan!* He didn't come here with his parents but as a representative of his entire race, and yet one who left that race as an infant. He's an infant who knows he's from somewhere, but knows precious little about where he's from compared to where he's landed. The problem—and the challenge—and the opportunity—is that *he is free to invent his own history.* Moreover, as an orphan, he *has to* invent his own history, since the one thing he does know is: he is not from here. As Engle says: "Orphans aren't merely free to reinvent themselves. They are *obliged* to do so."

So the dual identity is perhaps Superman's greatest wish fulfillment aspect, more so than flying or bending steel in his bare hands. He is able to cherry pick from the best both societies have to offer. His powers, which he actually only attained because he came to Earth—on Krypton, he and his people had none—mark him as the exceptional immigrant. Whatever objectionable qualities Kryptonians may have, they are none of his problem. He left there as a baby. He's not a bug-eyed monster-type alien—he's an alien who looks like the rest of earth humans. (And a handsome one, at that, modeled as he was on John Barrymore.) He can fit in when he wishes and distance himself when he wishes. He can use what he's learned as Kent to enhance his life as Superman, and vice versa.

Again, would we not all like to integrate all the sides of our personalities to, as the psychologists would put it, become one "fully realized" person? Ironically, Superman becomes integrated by splitting himself. That can be a comforting thought: *our dilemma is its own solution! Unity equals duality!* It's a neat trick, and one we actually do live with daily.

As an immigrant, Kent/Superman evinces that ambivalence one would expect. After all, if Superman truly wanted to blend in would he enter a profession—journalism—where courage is necessary, yet continually act in a cowardly way—but always get the scoop? How much more conspicuous could a person become in a role allegedly chosen to enable him to walk among us inconspicuously? The simultaneous needs to blend in and to stand out, echoing the immigrant's insecurities and self-confidence, are there in the Man of Steel.

Needless to say, when the Superman mythology was created, no one was imagining a serious discussion of these issues some 65 years later, and perhaps it isn't fair to scrutinize such a creation so closely. By the same token, that very lack of self-consciousness may enable us to read cultural signposts that would be harder to discern in a cultural vein more knowingly developed. One thing we can say that separates

Superman's dual identity from most others is this: Superman is the "real" person. Clark Kent is the fake. For most superheroes—with the exception of Wonder Woman and, in later years, the heroes derived from Asgardian and other pantheons—the *civilian* is the real, with the addition of powers, skills, magic or technology being what creates the heroic identity. Batman was the first in the endless procession of comics superheroes with extra identities grafted onto their identity bestowed at birth.

Is there a significant difference between the two types of secret identities? It would seem so. If you adapt an identity to disguise who you really are, so that you can have a "normal" life and a regular job, so you can have a respite from the unasked-for responsibility your power brings you, maybe that's understandable. Who would want to be incessantly bothered by people wanting their car towed or that unsightly tree stump pulled out of their front yard? Even Superman needs a break, if not a rest.

But what of the folks—the vast majority of heroes—whose civilian identities are the real ones? Are they more noble—and their villainous counterparts more ignoble—because they have a choice in what they do, and choose to do the right (or wrong, in the case of the villains) thing? After all, one can imagine that there must be plenty of people with amazing, superhuman abilities who keep it to themselves. They may be so unnerved by the power they've gained or the indestructible armor they've designed that that just want to put the whole thing out of their minds. Such was the conceit of the M. Night Shamayilan film *Unbreakable.*

Is it braver to be who you are, or to be who you *pretend* you are? This is the fundamental question of identity. The superhero asks the question in capital letters with triple question marks at the end of the sentence. Other questions, equally daunting, are suggested by the first: Who am I? Who would I like to be? Who would those I love like me to be? Who would those I hate like me to be? Who am I capable of being? Who must I be? And who says so?

The superhero's answers to these questions are generally: "I will be who I must be in order to fulfill my mission of doing good works. Whatever serves that purpose is who I will be both in and out of my costume." Whatever other annoying questions they may have—which echo our own quandaries—are quieted by this allegiance to duty. This may be the key to the societal identity crises the heroes reflect. For the superhero, the answer to the contradictory needs is: "Don't be selfish. Serve the community and the rest will fall into place. Who am I? I am the mechanism for perfecting and serving society. *And I know exactly what actions I must take to do that.*"

Wouldn't it be nice to know so clearly the right thing to do at the right time? To have to deceive and dissemble regarding something as intrinsic one's own identity in order to achieve the good seems a small price to pay. And in a fictional superhero's universe, with its clear parameters of moral correctness, it is no contradiction for lying to equal truth and honor. Again, we wish this were true in real life. We wish every one of our lies was done in the service of a greater purpose—not merely to get us out of unpleasant or inconvenient situations.

So the secret identity becomes, in the care of the superhero, a badge of honor instead of a concealment of shame. The real world vigilante becomes the fictional dispenser of justice. The secret identity accompanies the ability to know who needs punishing and just how much, and what type of, punishing they need.

The quantity of disguise is unimportant. One may be fooled by Spider-Man's full-face covering mask, but Superman? Even Batman and Captain America, with their half-face concealing masks, wouldn't fool anybody for long. And once they opened their mouths to speak, who could have any doubt who they were, never mind such telltale clues as body or cologne odor, aftershave, mouthwash, telltale scratches or moles, missing teeth, and so on. The conventions of the genre make it enough for most heroes—and villains—merely to *will* it that their identities be impenetrable, though those conventions also make it necessary that they make some kind of effort at deception. Once the effort is made, the rules of logic become malleable.

Over the decades, the role of the secret identity has become less significant in the comics themselves. One of the byproducts of the greater insistence on certain types of "realism" in superhero fiction has been that, the more "real" the characters become, the sillier the idea of the dual identity—at least the one concealed by a pair of glasses or a mask no more feature-distorting than a pair of glasses—has come to seem.

Marvel's Fantastic Four was the first to break down this tradition in Stan Lee and Jack Kirby's comparatively more realistic take on superheroes that ushered in the 1960s. But even they were to prove the exception, as Spider-Man, Iron Man, Thor, and most of the Marvel pantheon adopted dual identities and had many story lines that hinged on the existence of the dualities. Iron Man pretended to be the bodyguard of his civilian persona, Tony Stark, and spent a good while, when trapped in the armor for various reasons, being accused of murdering Stark. It seemed the audiences insisted that a superhuman adventurer be torn between two lives.

More and more in current comics the secret identity is at least severely compromised—the number of people who know Peter Parker is Spider-Man and Bruce Wayne is Batman must surely be in the triple digits by now—or ignored altogether. Do the X-Men in the comics have secret identities? One would be hard pressed to say for sure. It's an issue that often seems to be sidestepped in the printed adventures of the mutant sales sensations.

But in the current screen incarnations of the characters—the ones more familiar to the general public—the secret identity is alive and well. The Spider-Man of the movies is Peter Parker, and not even his girlfriend Mary Jane Watson knows that, despite her having kissed both Spider-Man and Peter. The X-Men are certainly unknown to the rest of the world. Daredevil's face is masked so even Elektra didn't catch on until late in the game. Batman and Superman, whether in movies, or on live or animated television, are definitely dual in their identities. TV versions of characters like Static and the Justice League (whose members, besides Superman, are Flash, Hawkgirl, Green Lantern, Wonder Woman, and Martian Manhunter) are secret-I.D. folks. It just seems that this is what the public wants—and needs—from its superheroes. The appeal of the secret identity is as primal as ever. Don't underestimate me. I may not be who you think I am. Or to put it another way:

IF ONLY THEY (*whoever your "they" may be*) KNEW THE TRUTH (*whatever that truth may be*) ABOUT ME (*whoever you believe yourself to be*), THEY'D BE SORRY FOR THE WAY THEY TREAT ME.

That's a powerful fantasy and a powerful human need. It's what makes people read and watch works of fiction. In some cases, it's what enables us to function on a daily basis. "This may seem like my life—but it is *not* my life. In my true life, I fly above buildings, I lift trucks in my bare hands, I defend the defenseless, and I am true to my truest self."

Maybe the "new realism" in the comics themselves is missing an important point that isn't lost on the creators of superhero fare for the screen. In the frenzy to get closer to some simulation of realism, perhaps an important part of the superhero fantasy is lost. The fantasy is a large part of what draws people to these heroes in the first place. After all, if a hero's identity is secret . . . then that cute guy or girl you've glanced across a crowded room may just think you are a Woman of

Wonder or a Super Man. Maybe that possibility even gives you the momentary illusion/fantasy/thrill that you could indeed be superpowerful. Of course, the illusion and the fantasy are fleeting and momentary and then all parties remember that this is the real world and that there are no superhumans.

But maybe . . . just maybe . . . .

4

Storm of the Orphans
Superman, Batman, and Spider-Man

Sherlock Holmes took to detection as a protest against the monotony of existence. Batman takes the same course out of an obsessive need to expunge his guilt and failure to toward his parents.

What makes Batman so different from Superman is that his character is formed by confronting a world which refuses to make sense. His experiences have taught him to be wholly cynical—yet he continues to risk life and limb in a one-man war against crime.

All Batman's most effective scripters and artists have understood that this madness is a part of Batman's special identity, and that the protagonist's obsessive character links him with his enemies in a more personal way than, say, Superman.

Richard Reynolds

"Bill and I had discussed it, and we figured there's nothing more traumatic than having your parents murdered before your eyes."

Bob Kane, creator of Batman, as quoted in
Batman: The Complete History, by Les Daniels

Psychologists say that it's a common if transient daydream among children to be rid of their parents, but having it actually come true is the stuff of nightmares.

Les Daniels, *DC Comics: Sixty Years of the
World's Favorite Comic Book Heroes*

W HAT, as Bob Kane so matter-of-factly comments, could be more terrible than violently losing your parents at an early age?

The answer is "nothing."

Such a loss leaves one alone and defenseless in the world, psychologically if not also physically. If, as Kane and co-creator Bill Finger, had figured, making Batman an orphan would "evoke sympathy for him," they certainly got their wish in spades. Oddly enough, it wasn't until several months after Batman first appeared that his origin was created and told. It was, as Daniels says, "an afterthought." But what an afterthought. Almost as if the whole orphan concept was too loaded to deal with.

But of all the orphaned superheroes—starting with Superman, whose success inspired DC Comics management to urge Bob Kane to create another costumed hero—there is no doubt that Batman was, until Spider-Man, the most traumatically affected by his orphan status.

One of the keys to the popularity of masked adventurers is the "they could be me" aspect, especially in the case of a character like Batman who, allegedly, is a normal human, trained to the peak of his abilities. But Batman is fueled by a rage against criminals and an unquenchable thirst for vengeance. Is that a wish-fulfillment fantasy? Indeed. And a powerful one. Who doesn't want payback for injustices committed against oneself?

When Superman punches an adversary's face, no matter how powerful that adversary, all he sees is the criminal's face. Orphan though he may be, Superman is the "sole survivor of a doomed planet." There was nothing personal in the death of his parents.

When Batman punches a foe, he sees the face of the man who killed his parents and left him—both mercifully and cruelly—as a seven-year-old wailing to the unheeding emptiness of the Gotham City night. Again, whether one accepts the act as random, or as personally tied to a scheme against his parents, as has been established in various comics stories, or even as *directly* connected to the origin of the character's prime villain—as shown in the 1989 Batman movie, where the Joker is revealed to have been the killer of the Waynes—all that the child knows is that an uncaring—or worse, a hostile—world has taken his protectors and nurturers from him in a cruel and abrupt manner.

One could argue that having such a dramatic change in one's life makes it harder to relate to a reading and viewing public. Most people's traumas are of a less extreme nature. But when a character has survived our worst fears, perhaps that is what truly makes him or her "relatable."

Apparently, the formula was thought so essential to Batman that Robin was introduced. Robin, too, was the victim of crime. His parents were murdered by criminals extorting the owners of the circus the family performed in as trapeze artists the Flying Graysons. Yet, Robin seems to have little of the bitter angst that fuels Batman. Aside from how depressing it would be to have *two* obsessed characters fighting side by side, there are reasons for this. For one, Robin has Batman, a figure who has stood in his shoes, to help him along through the difficult times ahead, to give him a purpose: in fighting crime in general, and avenging his loved ones' murders, in particular.

More significant, perhaps, is the fact that Robin's parents died for a *reason*. A selfish, venal criminal reason, true, but a *cause*, of which their death was an *effect*. A greedy person wanted money and their death served to frighten someone else into giving him money. To young Bruce, Thomas and Martha Wayne's deaths seemed to be *without* rhyme or reason. A death like that would only lead a young boy to feel responsible for not protecting them, and perhaps even that their deaths were his fault. Such was the case with the twice-orphaned Spider-Man, who lost his parents before he was born. Then—most significant to the young Peter Parker—came the murder of his beloved uncle, a death that came about due to circumstances which, with only a little twisting of logic, Peter became convinced were indirectly of his doing.

One must ask the question, of course: Where were the social and family safety net structures when Bruce was orphaned? Why was a young boy allowed to live on his own in a large mansion, attended only by Alfred, the family butler? Why wasn't the kid trundled off to live with some relative, well-to-do or otherwise? No doubt a survey would find some story line where this issue was dealt with, but it is really not a part of the Batman mythos anyone remembers. What people remember is the orphan, left alone with but an employee, rearing himself, and not just rearing himself, but becoming the world's greatest detective, as well as an extraordinary athlete, scientist, industrialist, and social butterfly.

That's a great fantasy: alone, with no help from anyone, you become tops in a variety of fields . . . and have a *second* job as the scourge of criminals everywhere, with the occasional trip to outer space to save the galaxy with Superman and the rest of your Justice League teammates.

Further, on a fantasy level, and hence on a commercial one, the trade-off in believability between an orphaned or nonorphaned character would seem rather clear, as well. After all, how else would one explain the incredible appeal to Americans and other democratic nonBritons of the stories of Princess Diana—and in a previous era, of the Duke and Duchess of Windsor—than to cite the seductive nature of the possibility, as in the most classic fairy tales, that we could be royalty and not know it—and that our petty lives would be rescued from the mundane by a simple revelation: *our parents are not really our parents.* There must have been some mistake. We must have been switched at birth in the maternity ward. Or our real parents—who were no doubt royalty, or superspies, or disease-cure-discovering Curies—were killed by criminals or kidnapped, or perhaps put in the witness protection program.

To be an orphan means that our possibilities are endless. We are not from the small town, the confining neighborhood, the constricting ethnic roots that we have been told are ours. We could be the King of England, the scions of industrial wealth.

We could become Batman if we were good enough. Not have to do math homework. Not have to look both ways before crossing the street.

Further, if one is an orphan, especially one without any seeming family ties, one is free, in the fantasy conception of such things, to do and go as one pleases. No father from whom to beg the car keys. No mother to denigrate the qualities of the friends with whom we associate. No annoying siblings with whom to vie for parental attention.

Really, whose mother would allow her child to be Batman or Robin, anyway?

Of course, in the real world, the psychological and economic realities of being an orphan are extraordinarily difficult to overcome. Trauma is by definition devastating to one's well-being and sense of stability. And benign neglect is still neglect. Waiting for the letter that tells us we are really princes and princesses in disguise becomes a fairly unpleasant exercise beyond the first couple of hours.

But to indulge in that fantasy while reading or watching the adventures of Batman can be an entrée into a version of ourselves that is extremely appealing. The superhero avatar enables us to be victim and protector at the same time. We get to save ourselves!

As previously noted, there have been endless speculations and discussions (beginning with Wertham) whether Batman and Robin are a gay fantasy, and what that means as subtext to their adventures. The existence of such a fantasy and its meanings are pretty much in the eye of the beholder. Certainly, one would be hard pressed to say that this was the intention of the characters' original creators. What seems a much more serious byproduct of their relationship is the willingness of Batman to take on a young child as a partner in fighting crime.

After all, it's one thing for a grown man to decide he's going to use his inherited wealth to engage in a war on crime, and to constantly risk his life in so doing. It's another to put a boy not even ten years old in the way of that same harm, no matter how enthusiastically the child may want to be part of the crime-fighting world. Certainly, a man such as Bruce Wayne, whose childhood was in effect stolen from him by the death of his parents, would want to protect other children from needless suffering. And yet, Batman hesitates only to the slightest degree.

Clearly, the public didn't mind. Batman's comics sales doubled with the introduction of Robin. And today, it is difficult to imagine the existence of Batman without Robin, who was introduced within the first year of Batman's own debut.

According to Jerry Robinson, a Kane collaborator who introduced many elements of the Batman mythos, as quoted in the Daniels *Batman* book: "It was Bob [Kane]'s idea to give Batman a kid sidekick. He wanted someone the young readers could identify with more readily than this masked, mysterious figure."

Daniels continues:

> *According to Kane, however, publisher Jack Liebowitz was skeptical about the idea of throwing a mere boy into harm's way, and from a realistic perspective he had a point. But Batman and Robin were fantasy figures, and readers responded enthusiastically to the death-defying kid.—37*

Perhaps Daniels holds the key to why Robin was and is considered an acceptable role model here in his brief referral to Robin as that "death-defying kid." In a fantasy world as defined by 1940s-era standards, there was no real worry that anything untoward of a permanent nature would happen to Dick Grayson.

And while, as with so much of the superhero mythologies, the stories were spawned from a simpler world, where people—children especially—were expected to suspend their disbelief in ways that wouldn't get in the way of a good story, in looking back with the benefit of hindsight, we have to see what we can learn from these common threads of the orphaned hero as well as the "kid" sidekick.

Even heroes who didn't have sidekicks had child or teen versions of themselves. Superboy, Kid Flash, Speedy (the Green Arrow's sidekick), Aqualad, were all expressions of the same desire to see a youthful version of, or counterpart to, the adult hero's existence. Indeed, it wouldn't be until the 1960s, with the X-Men, Spider-Man, and the Teen Titans— as well as the teens of Scooby Doo—that it was considered commercially viable for teenagers to carry their own titles. Although kid characters—mostly from the drawing board of Captain America and Bucky's creators Joe Simon and Jack Kirby—such as the *Boy Commandos* and the eponymous kids of *Boys' Ranch* were able to band together to do good, they certainly did not become the cultural icons that the sidekick kids of the 1940s became.

The prime appeal of the orphan myth, though, seems fairly consistent. Be it the orphan from another planet, like Superman, or the victim of circumstance, like Batman, the need—like the need expressed by the ubiquitous secret identity—is to know that you are not who people think you are. Indeed, the orphan element can be seen in some ways as an offshoot of the secret-identity mythos.

Not only is an orphan a tabula rasa—someone who could be anyone—who therefore expresses the message that you could be more than the mundane person you appear, but the orphan—in fantasy—need obey no rules beyond his own code, a code that is created from the visceral *evidence* of his own experience, and enforced by his ability to enforce that code.

Like modern-day rappers who feel the need to establish street cred, even if they grew up in well-to-do, middle class surroundings, some comics creators felt the need to mythologize their own lives, and in so doing give credence and authenticity to their creations. The great artist and writer Jack Kirby—who was instrumental in the creation of Captain America, the X-Men, the Fantastic Four, and the Hulk, among many others—often spoke of growing up on the streets of New York's Lower East Side, fighting and clawing his way to survival as he wrote and drew his way to respectability and a home studio on Long Island and ultimately in suburban Thousand Oaks, California. No doubt the kernels of Kirby's stories were true—certainly his death-defying combat experiences in World War II have never been contradicted—and no doubt he had his share of streetfights on the Lower East Side—but it is the *myth* of the street kid, the urchin battling for every inch of turf, that fueled Kirby's imagination and drive. To him, every day was a struggle, a Darwinian fight for space and light. Although he has recounted loving and tender memories of his family, one can imagine the future King of Comics feeling most alive when on those streets, not having to answer to anyone, being the individual at war with a hostile world. No mother calling him for supper. No father reading him a bedtime story. He, one boy, creating himself into the man who would emerge daily to slay the dragons of the world, whatever form they may take; the urban cowboy, each day reaffirming his status as top gun, or at least as a survivor.

That's the side to which the orphan myth plays. The idea, so emphasized and mythologized in American popular culture is: we are all alone. We fight our own battles, make our own rules, defy those who would destroy us. We are alone to succeed or fail, to triumph or suc-cumb.

We make our own destinies.

And while the inhabitants of the real world we live in become ever more interdependent, the cult of the individual becomes more and more important in our fantasies. This is the need the *Matrix* movies tap. In *The Matrix*, all humanity—except for a chosen few who have liberated themselves—are literal slaves to the computers that rule the world, while existing in a computer-induced illusion that they have free will. The chosen few who indeed have free will—along with the burdens that freedom brings with it—are the ultimate last free men and women. Whereas those who sleep within the Matrix have the illu-sion of individual freedom (the legacy of the old frontier myths like those of the Virginian and Buffalo Bill) while being slaves to the worst aspects of collective consciousness, those who are truly free ultimately fight *alone*. Which is preferable? Our instincts tell us to be alone and aware, with the perhaps distant hope of building a community. Even if we fail at building it, or its goals are never realized, we still know that we have tried. We'd rather be alone—orphans—on our own terms than be taken care of if it is as slaves to a government or a machine, or even an idea.

Which opens the question: Is the idea of freedom a mass delusion? Or phrased more positively, is it a hope that people hold, a hope that is embodied in the paradoxical freedom of the orphan?

Consider the case of the biblical Moses. Cast adrift from his Hebraic roots by a family seeking to save his life, he is found by Pharaoh's daughter, and reared as her own. In a twist on many of the orphan leg-ends we are fond of, Moses is found by royalty and so reared, only to discover his own special nature—special beyond being a Prince of

Egypt—in being the one chosen to lead his people (who he does not yet realize are his people) out of bondage and into nationhood. Still, the transforming power of orphanhood is key to unleashing the potential of the jettisoned baby.

Interestingly, Jesus is not an orphan. The support of his family is central to the development of the biblical character. (Although, of course, to somewhat hew to the orphan theme, Jesus is reared by a foster father. His "real" father, in heaven, puts his savior son through trials and tests, resulting in crucifixion and climaxing in resurrection.) So, for all his "normal" upbringing, Jesus certainly is not the product of a two-cars-in-the-garage family, or the ancient Bethlehemian equivalent.

And how could he be? How can a hero, an iconic figure, be prey to the petty concerns of everyday life? Could Batman do his job if he were to get a call from his wife reminding him to bring home a quart of milk? How can Superman defend the solar system if he has to go to parent-teacher night and argue about why Kal-El Jr. only got a C on his English paper? More to the point, relating to his own parentage, can a super-hero be expected to make time for his or her folks? Will Mom feel neglected if he has to divert a flooding river when he's promised to help her polish her silverware?

Significantly, the Superman legend—as exemplified by the popular *Smallville* television series—answers in the affirmative. Although he has lost his Kryptonian parents, Clark Kent is very much the son of Jonathan and Martha Kent. They transmit cornfed rural values to this survivor of a doomed technological civilization, one not unlike the world of *The Matrix*.

Over the years, the Kents' role in the Superman mythos has changed. Early in the creation of the character's history, they were shown to have died at some undetermined point, leaving Clark doubly orphaned. Then, as time went on, they were shown to be alive in Clark's adolescence, much as they are in the *Smallville* series today. So it would seem, for Superman at least, being a full-on orphan—with no parental figures at all—is sometimes all right, depending on the needs of the times. Some eras will tolerate—or insist—on a Superman with living foster parents. Others will demand a Man of Steel who fights his battles alone. Since Superman has come to embody (more so, really, than even Captain America) the ideals and values of America—hard work, fair play, the opportunity to maximize your potential—it seems right that, as in the case of the secret identity, he sets the pace for all the others.

It is notable that Spider-Man mixes elements of both the Batman and the Superman mythos to create a unique blend that in many ways ushered the solo superhero into the modern age. Spider-Man is originally presented to us as an orphan, but one whose parents perished under unrevealed circumstances. In a rare misstep, it was before long revealed that they were secret agents who perished in service to America. This was an attempt to adhere to the orphan mythos trope that says: "My real parents were special." But it also removes from Peter Parker the important Everyman aspect. In general, the spy aspect of his parents' lives has been downplayed. It's enough to know he was orphaned and not abandoned, and taken in—if not fully adopted—by his father's brother, Ben, and Ben's wife, May. Ben and May had no children, and treated Peter as their own son, if not like a grandson, given how much older Ben and May seemed than Richard and Mary, and how they doted on him so unconditionally.

So Spider-Man's was the trauma of a child orphaned—or half-orphaned—a *second* time by the murder of Ben shortly after Peter acquired his spider-powers. While off doing what any teenager with such abilities would do—showing off and making money with his powers—Peter neglected to stop a thief, who would then go on to be the one who murdered his uncle. Peter found and captured the killer—but it was a hollow victory. The crime had been, like the murder of Batman's parents, seemingly random. Later revisions would consider the randomness or lack thereof, but in the popular imagination the idea will always be that of a random act.

Yet here is a random act that only took place because Peter had selfishly let the thief escape that first time. Here, Peter learned that "with great power there must also come great responsibility." One can argue if the lesson is warranted or not, or just signs of the twice-traumatized orphan boy's need to wrest responsibility for his beloved uncle's death to at least proclaim some control—even of the most negative kind—over his life, a control he had no hope of exerting when his parents died, far from home, under mysterious circumstances, when he was barely old enough even to understand what had befallen them, and him.

In his origin, Spider-Man found Ben's killer—a burglar he had selfishly not pursued at an earlier point—and defeated him, then left him, webbed-up, for the police. The criminal was captured. The system could then work its impartial justice on the murderer. There was no mysterious killer, fleeing in the twilight. Who, then, was Peter Parker to seek revenge on?

After all, in the case of Batman, the child Bruce Wayne was traumatized into a lifelong search for vengeance and closure by becoming a scourge of crime, and to eventually—almost by chance—bring his parents' killer to justice. And Superman has no murderous force who made him an orphan—perhaps the reason why his view of the Universe is so much more benign, despite his having seen evil in a hundred galactic settings, despite his super-keen senses making him aware of the slightest wrong being done at any time. Superman's quest is to use the power of Krypton and the values of Smallville to do good. Spider-Man's quest is the most difficult and perilous of all the orphan quests.

Because Spider-Man is seeking revenge on *himself.*

No matter how many symbolic stand-ins for the burglar he defeats, it will never be enough for him. Indeed, Peter Parker's internalization of his guilt over his perceived culpability in his uncle's death can be defined as classic neurotic behavior. The annals of Spider-Man's history show how, despite his obvious courage, integrity, selflessness, and determination, he has a compulsion to get in his own way. Far from the modesty of the Lenny Bruce Masked Man, Spider-Man is obsessed with finding the *bad* in whatever good he does.

This is not to say that Spider-Man is a humorless, obsessed character. That distinction goes to Batman, and, more pathologically, to the Punisher, more about whom shortly. Spider-Man actually functions on at least two levels. He's probably the wittiest and drollest of superheroes. Both as Peter Parker and as Spider-Man, he's a very funny guy, almost a Seinfeld with webbing. Peter has many reasons to be Spider-Man, each of which he believes to be the most important, depending on the context and on his mood. The outrage of the orphan—at both the cruel world and at his all-too-human self—is but one of these reasons. The others include: making money taking photos of himself for the *Daily Bugle,* and just plain having fun. (It is, after all, fun to be Spider-Man— as it is to be Superman and even Batman. If it wasn't, who would relate to their adventures at all?)

In his most serious moments, of course, Spider-Man will say that he is Spider-Man to make up for the mistake he made. But the thing that makes Parker so modern—and so human—is not merely the combination of emotions that spur him on, and hence his multiple motivations, but that he, despite being an iconic figure featured on pajamas and Slurpee cups, is like all of us, capable of encompassing contradictions. As Walt Whitman says in "Song of Myself": "Do I contradict myself? Very well then I contradict myself." Peter is an orphan with the ability,

unlike Batman, to step outside of himself and say: "Hey, it may be life
and death—but life's too short to not have some fun, too."

Another twist on the orphan myth, a twist which makes Spider-Man
the progenitor of the third heroic-orphan vein, is his take on responsibility. While his Aunt May continued to take care of him, as the Kents
did with Clark, and Alfred and various corporate entities did with
Bruce Wayne, indeed as Bruce Wayne did with Dick Grayson, supporting and training him as he became Robin, the Boy Wonder, it was more
often Peter who was taking care of her.

This was the classic Spider-Man dilemma, brilliantly portrayed by
Lee and Ditko in what has come to be called "The Master Planner
Saga." In this paradigmatic Spider-Man story, the same item—a radioactive isotope—that the villain needs to achieve his plan for domi-
nation is the same vial of material that Aunt May needs to be cured of
radiation poisoning—a condition she found herself in because of a
transfusion Peter selflessly gave her from his radioactive blood. Peter's
life, it seems, often ends up with his being the danger as much as being
the savior. As a metaphor for modern life, what could be more perfect?
Progress leads to pollution. Cleaning up pollution leads to graft in ap-
portioning contracts for the cleanups. But the contracts create much-
needed jobs . . . and so on.

Further, Peter more often than not takes care of his aunt financially.
Constantly ill and underinsured, unable to make a living beyond her
Social Security payments, it is Peter's earnings as a photographer that
enables her to survive. (Truth be told, even on the fateful night of Ben's
murder, Peter was out performing as Spider-Man, mostly so he could
earn money to help out his aunt and uncle.) With no Wayne fortune or
Kent farm, Peter Parker is the orphan who, far from being rescued,
must do the rescuing. Not only must he redeem himself, he must save

the world in general and his aunt in particular, especially since she embodies his last connection to his parents and his uncle. Peter alternately—sometimes even simultaneously—feels like he's ten feet tall and two inches high. What we normally think of as how a child, even an adolescent, should be treated is turned on its head. The ideal pattern is one in which the child is taken care of until, gradually, he can take care of himself. Eventually, the grown child will go out on his own, perhaps returning when his parents are in their old age to help them out, morally and spiritually if not financially. In the case of Spider-Man, the orphan becomes the parent, the victim the caretaker.

Way on the other end of the orphan spectrum and of the orphan equation is the angriest orphan of all: the Punisher. Not as popularly known as Batman, perhaps because his history and worldview are so bleak, Frank Castle is a sort of reverse orphan. While picnicking in Central Park with his wife and children, Castle's family is caught in the crossfire of an underworld gang war. Castle alone survives. He swears to eradicate criminals everywhere. Castle's loss—in its way a kind of orphan's tragedy—becomes fuel for rage and violence. Inspired by the Charles Bronson *Death Wish* movies, which were themselves responses to the sense of crime-out-of-control of the 1970s and 1980s, the Punisher added the superhero comic twist to the films' formula. While non-superpowered—unless one counts the ability to not kill scores of innocent civilian bystanders while machine-gunning and grenading hordes of criminals—the Punisher addressed another aspect of the angry orphan. Equipped with heavy-duty high-tech weaponry, Castle set out on his one-man war on crime.

Generally more a cipher than a person, the Punisher took the rage and grief of Batman and ratcheted it up to the highest degree. Would all the killing bring his, or anyone's, loved ones back? Of course not. Would his quest strike a chord with audiences? For a time, certainly, in much the same way Bronson's or Clint Eastwood's *Dirty Harry* movies did.

The orphan condition, in its extreme and idealized versions, feeds a large part of what we look for and find satisfying in superhero mythology. One could argue that, while the fantasy appeals to a large and diverse audience, it typically ignores certain fantasies and concerns of girls and women, as well as the fantasies of those who need and want stories of families.

As we will see, the superhero mythos is a large tent, and it has ample room for those needs, too.

5

Amazon Grace

Wonder Woman, Xena, and Buffy

*It seemed to me, from a psychological angle, that the comics' worst of-
fense was their blood-curdling masculinity. . . . It's smart to be strong.
It's big to be generous, but it's sissified, according to exclusively male
rules, to be tender, loving, affectionate, and alluring. "Aw, that's girl
stuff!" snorts our young comics reader, "Who wants to be a girl?"
And that's the point: not even girls want to be girls so long as our fem-
inine archetype lacks force, strength. . . . Women's strong qualities
have become despised because of their weak ones.*

William Moulton Marston, creator of Wonder Woman,
The American Scholar, 1943, as quoted by Trina Robbins in
The Great Women Superheroes

*I designed Buffy to be an icon, to be an emotional experience, to be loved
in a way that other shows can't be loved. Because it's about adolescence,
which is the most important thing people go through in their development, becoming an adult. And it mythologizes it in such a way, such a
romantic way—it basically says, "Everybody who made it through adolescence is a hero."*

Joss Whedon, interviewed by Joe Nazzaro in *Writing Science
Fiction and Fantasy Television*

WHEN Superman smashes an enemy's super weapon to bits, we cheer. When Batman slings his bat-rope and snares a fleeing killer, yanking him savagely to the ground, we thrill that, at least in fantasy, good has triumphed through violence. And when Buffy shoves her spike—aka Mr. Pointy—through the heart of a vampire stalking a helpless teenage girl, we're happy to see evil taken out of the picture. We wish we could be her. Whether we're man or woman, boy or girl. Her victory is our victory as much as Superman's and Batman's are.

This is a relatively new phenomenon: the powerful woman who is also a good "guy." Up until the 1990s, in pop culture, if a woman was powerful—*really* powerful—she was either evil, or made evil by the power.

While women surgeons were performing organ transplants, while women lawyers were winning multimillion dollar cases, while women executives were leading at least a few Fortune 500 companies—Wonder Woman was . . . what was she doing, anyway? Whatever it was, it certainly wasn't of interest to most pop-culture lovers.

Maybe we, as a society, just weren't ready for a superhuman woman who could be good and powerful at the same time. Women in pop culture always seemed like they could be one or the other. With the notable exception of Wonder Woman, who was good and was powerful, there hadn't been a successful, superheroine who was *femme* but not *fatale*, pretty much until Buffy. Even Warrior Princess Xena had been, in many ways, the anti-Wonder Woman. With a trail of bodies left behind from her marauding days, Xena had a lot for which to atone.

And, hey—Xena? Buffy? They were never even in comics until they had established themselves on the tube. True, that's part of the eternal cross-pollination between media for which pop culture icons, especially superpowered ones, are famous. But it does seem notable that for superwomen it's the norm, not the exception, not to start out on the printed page.

The fact that superheroes have more often than not appealed to male youthful power fantasies than to women's seems like the easy answer. Of course, which came first: the Phoenix or the egg? (Phoenix, for those not in the know, was a major female superheroine of the 1970s—whose great power led her to became a supervillain. She destroyed a solar system and laughed about it!) Were there so few female superheroes who transcended genre because they didn't strike a chord in popular consciousness? Or did they not strike that chord because they didn't exist?

In *The Great Comic Book Heroes*, Jules Feiffer famously puts it this way:

> *My problem with Wonder Woman was that I could never get myself to believe she was that good. . . . Wonder Woman seemed more like too much of a put up job, a fixed comic strip—a product of group thinking rather than the individual inspiration that created Superman. . . . Nobody's heart was in it. It was choppily written and dully drawn. . . . Her violence was too immaculate, never once boiling over into a little fantasmal sadism.—45*

In other words, the original superheroines weren't allowed to be as over-the-top as their male counterparts, but no one was able to figure out just what to do with them. At least villainous superwomen—from Catwoman on—had the luxury of not having to fight the good fight. They just had to put up *a* good fight.

So if comic-book publishers weren't going to create the defining fantasy of powerful but good superheroines, it would be up to creators a few generations down the road to assimilate feminist attitudes into mainstream culture through the fact that both were so natural to them. Their mothers were doctors, their sisters, lawyers, their female cousins ran corporations. To this new generation, a woman could be in a position of power was not unusual or a "credit to her sex," but just the way things were.

These things *had* happened before, of course. During World War II, with many men off fighting, women took their places in all sorts of professions and jobs. But it was understood that when her fighting man came home, Rosie the Riveter would hand her riveting gun back over and pick up her frying pan and knitting needles again.

So, from Miss America—not the beauty queen, but the Timely/ Atlas/Marvel heroine of the 1940s to the Invisible Girl—a grown woman who, most of the time, was as visible as anybody else—to the She-Hulk (as unpoetic a name as ever tripped out of a comics caption)—there was always an awkwardness and self-consciousness to superheroines. Our society's ideals of fair play demanded there be superheroines. But our society's ingrained, conflicted, and unconscious feelings toward powerful women made the creation of truly crowd-pleasing superhero women take decades—generations—longer to develop than their male counterparts.

With the way led by superwomen in movies, evolution came slowly. It was almost as if generations of creative people had to enter the media industries, work, create, and then retire, while social changes buffeted the world around them, that pop culture was able to come around to the realization that, if men could be savagely, violently powerful in the service of Good, then so could women. Sarah Connor in the *Terminator* films, Ripley in the *Alien* movie mythos, and even Lara Croft in the *Tomb Raider* games (the inspiration, of course, for the films of the same title) were the first pop media women to show the way.

The current generation of adolescent boys love active, powerful, threatening female figures—often as protagonists and often . . . as a heroic surrogate for the boy himself . . .

Girls have long been known to identify with male fantasy figures. Now it looks as though young boys are finally learning the same art . . .

By combining the "frailties" normally allowed to women in commercial entertainment with the power and anger allowed to men, they become much more complete characters.

Gerard Jones. *Killing Monsters: Why Children Need Fantasy,*
Super-Heroes and Make-Believe Violence—160–61

Buffy is the ultimate realization of this evolutionary and revolutionary change in attitudes of, and attitudes about, female superheroes. She is a hybrid creation of several powerful veins of superhero literature that come together to form a potent myth for our times. These three are the superhero, the family metaphor, and the teen fantasy, where the group of committed friends and allies become the substitute for the family that cannot, or will not, understand what the hero and their allies must go through. Yet she is not, as say, Rogue or Shadowcat of the X-Men, a character who functions primarily as a member of a unit. She has a surrogate family, but she leads them. The others have a vote, but Buffy is the only one with a veto. (The notable exception to this statement came in the series' final story arc where, to move the plot in a certain direction, Buffy's veto power was removed, lessening, for this viewer, the dramatic impact of the story line.)

Significantly, Buffy is also the first superhero we are examining who did not emerge from the pages of comic books, but whose sensibilities, priorities, and values are cut from the same indestructible cloth, and feed from the same needs and desires of the most primal of superhero myths. Indeed, the series itself constantly references superhero comics, and has spun off into several versions of itself in the pages of published comics.

Buffy and her friends even refer to themselves as "the Scooby Gang," a direct reference to the adventurers in the *Scooby Doo* animated series, the live-action movie version of which actually starred Buffy, herself, Sarah Michelle Gellar. They could as easily— and actually have—referred to themselves as the Fantastic Four, the archetypal superhero family oriented team. For that matter, the Buffy team could be cousins to the various X-Men incarnations, more for their internal bickering and romantic attachments than for any single "freakishness" and prejudice metaphor as displayed by the mutant X-Men. If anything, the "persecuted" in Buffy could be seen as the vampires themselves, picked on and, well, slain just because they're different. Of course, they're different in the way that cancer cells are different. Their differences could spell the end of human life—which would be their downfall, too, since in a world ruled by vampires, there would be no one on whom the vampires could feed.

But let's look at Buffy for what is her most important aspect: the effect that gaining power has upon a teenager—and specifically a female teenager. A female teenager who, before finding out she was "the chosen one," was most concerned with the ephemera and trivialities of adolescent life in modern suburbia.

Buffy's origins, however, lie in the first and most famous of the comics superheroines, Wonder Woman. Superman, Batman, Captain America, and the Spirit were created by high-school educated men in their teens and twenties, making their way from the poor or lower-middle-class environs of their parents' homes, pretending—as much as their dual-identified creations pretended—to be mature, sophisticated men of the world.

Wonder Woman, on the other hand, was created by William Moulton Marston, Ph.D., a middle-aged, highly educated, highly accomplished adult. Harvard graduate Marston was a lawyer as well as a practicing psychologist. He was most famous as the inventor of the lie detector.

In his own secret identity, Marston engaged in an alternate lifestyle, offbeat even by today's standards. He was married to and had two children with his wife, psychologist Elizabeth Holloway Marston, and also had two more children with his assistant, Olive Byrne, who lived with the Marstons. By all accounts, all three adults got along quite well, and when Marston died, the two women together brought up the four children.

Marston was perhaps the first "pop" psychologist in history. According to Trina Robbins in her 1996 book *The Great Woman Super Heroes*, he was also "a successful advertising man, and the author of popular and scholarly books and articles on psychology." Other accounts, like Les Daniels in his book *Wonder Woman*—a book officially sanctioned by DC Comics—describe a man with great ups and downs in his financial fortunes, and who, depending on how it suited his needs, went from being an almost Wertham-like attacker of comics to a defender of them, going so far as to serve on DC Comics advisory board. Ultimately, Marston would become so involved with comics that he would create—with input from legendary DC executive M. C. Gaines (father of *Mad's* original publisher, William Gaines)—the first female superhero, the Amazon princess Wonder Woman. Still, from all accounts, he was widely liked and admired, including by his children.

Created in a virgin birth—rising from the dust—Wonder Woman came to life. She was birthed from dust, like Adam, the granddaddy of us all. No "Adam's rib" style, second-thought origin for her!

The mythic hero is usually born from the union of a virgin and a god, and when the virginal Amazon queen Hippolyta desires a child, the goddess Aphrodite instructs her to mold one out of clay, then breathes life into the statue. Thus, Wonder Woman's divine parent is, in this case, a female deity, and little Diana has two mommies.—Robbins, 7

Well versed in mythology and fairy tales, Marston (writing under the name Charles Moulton) was able to draw on these primal stories and, with a modern psychologist's sensibility, give them a twist for the audience of 1942. But like many of the heroes and heroines of her day, Wonder Woman swiftly became caught up helping the allies win World War II, which threatened her idyllic Amazon homeland on Paradise Island. When Steve Trevor, an intelligence officer for the US, crashes on Paradise and is nursed back to health by Princess Diana (Wonder Woman), he persuades her to come back to "man's world" with him and fight the good fight.

Like the Sub-Mariner over at Timely—later Marvel—Wonder Woman was able to take whatever ambivalence or outright hostility she might have felt about the world outside her cloistered environment and channel it into Axis bashing. In a sort of variant on Superman's immigrant status, Wonder Woman, too, is an immigrant from Paradise Island, and becomes a champion of the modern-day Paradise that is America in the eyes of the immigrants who flocked and continue to flock to its shores. The very theme of her costume with its red and blue, punctuated by white stars, is as American as . . . well, as spinach pie, to continue the metaphor of her Grecian origins.

At their 1940s height, Wonder Woman's comics sold millions of copies a month. Along with Superman and Batman, she was the only comics character whose adventures have been published continuously since her introduction several generations ago. Certainly, when most people are asked to name a superheroine, Wonder Woman would be the one they name.

Cultural critics like Gloria Steinem have been famously inspired by Wonder Woman. As Steinem says in her introduction to the 1995 *Wonder Woman: Featuring over Five Decades of Great Covers*:

The lesson [of Wonder Woman] was that each of us might have unknown powers within us, if we only believed and practiced them. . . . Perhaps that's the appeal of Wonder Woman . . . an adult's need for a lost balance between women and men, between humans and nature.—7, 19

Further, feminist and women's-studies professor Lillian S. Robinson comments in *ArtForum* (Summer 1989):

What enchanted me about Wonder Woman was her physical power. That it was enrolled in the good fight was taken sufficiently for granted that I could concentrate on the power itself . . .

Wonder Woman merged the natural and the supernatural, without reference to the extraterrestrial. She wasn't strong the way someone from Krypton would be . . . but she was skilled. She had developed her abilities to a fine, a martial art.—101

Wonder Woman was Rosie the Riveter writ large. Like Rosie, she had power—Rosie could hold the riveting gun, no mean feat in itself. But Rosie also had the *skill*—whether self-taught, taught by a male riveter, or by another *female* riveter—to use the tool skillfully. Wonder Woman—like Rosie—took her power and skill, and used it to, literally and figuratively, empower herself along with her readers, both female and male. Like Superman, Wonder Woman was the real character. Like Superman, a reader could experience her adventures and feel that, like Diana Prince with her real power hidden, the world would treat her differently if they only knew how powerful she really was.

And yet, there always seemed to be something "good for you" about Wonder Woman, as if she were created by a psychologist with a social agenda, as muddled and constantly evolving as that agenda might have been. And since, in a business famous for doing as little expensive demographic research as possible, it's hard to say if *Wonder Woman* was read, at its peak, by more boys than girls, or by more children than adults. Certainly, the quantity of "reboots" and re-imaginings of the character—she has been goddess, warrior, private eye, and much more—indicates that, while philosophically and commercially, the idea of having a major superheroine in play was certainly desirable and even admirable, nobody really knew what to do with her. Again, in the hypothetical woman-on-the-street interview, while everybody knows Wonder Woman, and many could even say she was an Amazon, how many people—how many people reading this very book—could encapsulate her origin the way they could those of Superman, Batman, and Spider-Man? With a very popular 1970s TV series and her famous appearance on the cover of the debut issue of Steinem's *Ms.* magazine, Wonder Woman is certainly an icon, an inspiration, and a role model—but not necessarily someone with whom you'd want to sit down for a meal. She seems pleasant but not really all that interesting.

Buffy would be fun to have dinner with.

Clearly, there are generations of women who were inspired, as Steinem and Robinson were, to a greater or lesser degree by Wonder Woman. No doubt there were many boys who became men with positive feelings about women that stem from Wonder Woman's adventures. But there isn't, it seems, the primal feeling about her that we have about so many of the Ur-male heroes. One part of it may be a societal unease, certainly in existence 60 years ago, about putting women in the traumatic positions into which popular culture puts men. Would the world of the 1940s have been able to make an icon of a woman whose parents were brutally murdered before her eyes the way it had of Batman? What about making a hero of a girl infant, rocketed from her doomed planet as the sole survivor the way Superman was? The very emotional savagery of the origins of the male icons, as opposed to the gentler, literally earthy beginnings of Wonder Woman, means that the men's beginnings would grab you by the throat and not let go. Wonder Woman's origin—birthed of and exuding good intentions—seems lacking in visceral drama the way the dread of orphandom and abandonment is thrust into a reader's face in the cases of Superman and Batman. It is the intense emotions these origin tales tap into that make them modern myths, as opposed to the trappings of myth in Wonder Woman's origin, but without the accompanying emotional terror that makes her primal impetus perhaps less compelling.

Wonder Woman's appearance on the comics scene was followed by if not a deluge, then at least a steady stream, of costumed female superheroes. Most of them are forgotten. Few of them went beyond comics into movies, radio shows, and TV series. Perhaps this is because the majority of superhero comics fans are boys and male teenagers who prefer their heroes like them, or some sort of version of who it is that they'd like to be. For this audience, it would take, apparently, a greater suspension of disbelief to imagine that a woman could be enacting your ambitions than that a man can fly.

Despite the profusion of female superheroes like Miss Fury (who technically predated Wonder Woman), Venus, and the Black Canary, probably the most famous superheroine was Mary Marvel, who was Billy Batson (Captain Marvel)'s twin sister. Tellingly, though the boy Billy became the adult Captain when he said *Shazam*, Mary became a super-powered child, and certainly had no title before her name.

Usually, the most well-known superhero women were spin-offs or sidekicks of their male counterparts, as with Mary Marvel. There were Batgirl, Batwoman, Namora (Namor the Sub-Mariner's cousin), and others. And while there were scores of female heroes, none of them captured the popular imagination after Wonder Woman claimed that niche. Everybody knew the Amazon princess, and her comics sold well, even if other females' did not.

It wasn't until the late 1950s that things started to change. With the introduction of Superman's long-lost cousin Kara, who would become Supergirl, the superheroine seemed to be a viable entity. Note that there already existed a Superboy, a super horse, a super dog and a super monkey! It took a lot of delay, apparently, for a Supergirl to be considered viable. Children of the 1950s and 1960s took to this character. She had a long run in various comics. But again, Supergirl would not get a movie until the 1980s. Something about a super-female couldn't make the leap from the printed page to mass consciousness until later. The *Supergirl* film was quickly forgotten, but at least she did make the move.

As noted, in the early 1960s Stan Lee's Marvel Comics revolutionized the field in many ways. Even then, though, the females were few and, more significantly, generally lower-powered than their male teammates. There was the Invisible Girl, Marvel Girl, the Wasp. These superheroines were always teammates. There were no solo Marvel superheroines until the 1970s, and no critical mass of them until the 1980s.

The most famous of the Marvel superheroines came from the pages of the X-Men franchise. Whereas Jean Grey—then known as Marvel Girl (no use of the dreaded "W" word here)—had started out her existence as a telekinetically powered hero who was prone to fainting spells, she eventually became a wielder of the "Phoenix force," which made her one of the cosmic-powered Marvel heroes, a near-deity on a power level with the Silver Surfer or even the Surfer's former boss, the planet-devouring Galactus.

Eventually—inevitably, given the societal view of powerful women—the Phoenix power turned Jean evil. She became Dark Phoenix (and the subject of darkness being associated with evil is the subject for a book beyond the scope of this one) and immediately set about killing billions of innocent alien beings. Much controversy was engendered within Marvel itself and within comics fandom when it was decreed that Jean must die for her crimes.

(Needless to say, as a comics hero—and gender makes no discrimination here—her death was temporary and she was brought back to life several years later, conveniently cleansed of her past sins, which were palmed off on the Phoenix entity, not Jean. A mixed message there, indeed. As a female, was she not thought worthy of being evil? Of course, if all she could be was evil, then was that not damning her entire sex?)

In the same era that birthed (and rebirthed) Phoenix, there was also born Elektra, who today is at her most popular, having been played by Jennifer Garner in the *Daredevil* movie and now being spun off into her own solo film franchise. Elektra was certainly the opposite of the helpless female and, like Phoenix, Elektra has died and come back to life any number of times. Unlike Phoenix, Elektra was a solo act—a feared and highly paid assassin for hire.

Again, one should note that, whereas Batman and Spider-Man would take personal tragedy and transform it into socially useful aggression, Elektra decides that the only way to make up for her own father's senseless murder is . . . to make a career of committing senseless murders! Even in the wake of the most influential feminist wave in history, a superhumanly powerful woman could only be powerful in the service of evil.

In their otherwise intelligent, thorough, and well-reasoned book, *The Myth of the American Superhero*, authors John Shelton Lawrence and Robert Jewett—even while savagely critiquing the superhero mythos as depicted in a variety of popular media—somehow neglect to mention Wonder Woman, or any superheroine, even once. There is mention of Heidi and Mary Poppins, but Wonder Woman, Supergirl, and She-Hulk merit not even a single sentence from this clearly pop-culture

savvy pair. No Buffy or Dark Angel, either. Not even a mention of Ripley from the *Alien* movies or of Linda Hamilton's Sarah Connor character from the *Terminator* films, two of the most recognizable female
adventurers in modern heroic fiction. No mention of Princess Leia from
Star Wars, not even easy targets like *Barb Wire* or *Tank Girl*, and not a
word on Xena.

Why would even scholarly treatises like *Myth* ignore the superheroine? How did Lawrence and Jewett—unafraid to blame superhero
culture for real-life characters like the Unabomber and Timothy
McVeigh—not find it in their agenda to mention any of the superwomen who swarm through our popular culture? One has to wonder if
the women just did not come up on the authors' radar. (This is not to
single these commentators out. The majority of male cultural critics do
not give much attention to these characters. Not surprising—the critics
are, after all, products of the culture they are examining.)

But as is clear by their longevity and popularity, superheroines feed
a cultural need. True, very few have had histories as long and sustained
as Superman, Batman, and Spider-Man. Wonder Woman, again, is the
only one in that category. No matter what her comics sales may have
been, anyone who knows there is a Superman also knows there is a
Wonder Woman. He or she may not know much about her, but they
know she exists.

Among the unique qualities of Buffy and Xena is that they are solo
characters who are not female versions of anybody. They are their own
women. Buffy may seem to function as a member of the aforementioned "Scooby Gang," but it is clear that they are supporting cast, not
peers. They all have their function, but the title of the series is *Buffy the
Vampire Slayer*, not *Buffy and Her Vampire Slaying Friends*. In the same
way that there is no Rolling Stones band without Mick Jagger, there is
no *Buffy* show without Buffy.

Xena, although spinning out of the *Hercules* series, is no "Lady Hercules." Indeed, given the Amazonian-mythological milieu that in many ways echoes Wonder Woman's, one could even say that Xena was an updated or revisited Wonder Woman, this time allowed to give free reign to the power and anger that the original never could.

The modern superheroine, as exemplified by Buffy, Xena, Ripley, and Sarah Connor, is allowed to be powerful and angry and in control. This new archetype is also allowed to cry and wear makeup and heels, and still credibly take on the most powerful forces of villainy.

And she does not have to be evil to be powerful.

Further, she does not have to be a lesbian to be powerful. But if she is a lesbian, that's fine, too. The universes of genre fiction reflect the times in which they are created. As society evolves, so does its fantasy life as refracted through popular culture.

Of course since so much of heroic popular culture is male-driven, and since many men are titillated by lesbianism, it's considered more than acceptable if a female superhero is gay. Our culture has come to the point where the lines between "grrl power" and exploitive PG-rated lesbian lovemaking, as in the case of Buffy's Dark Phoenix-like ally, the wiccan Willow, are blurry indeed. Certainly, while lesbianism is now fairly common on TV series and in movies, passionate scenes of men kissing men can be seen on *Six Feet Under, Queer as Folk* and . . . well, nowhere on network, non-cable TV.

But for the most part—with the notable exception of Xena—super-women have boyfriends or husbands, and live in societies where, as with their male counterparts, responsibility stands in their path like giant boulders, and they, as good people, cannot ignore it. We have gotten, finally, to the stage where a powerful woman can be taken on her own terms by men as well as by women, by boys and girls looking for role models. Do these women—even the gay ones—have to be sexy in a manner appealing to straight men and boys? Probably, if the producers wish to have as broad an audience as possible. But, as Gerard Jones notes:

> Buffy is a whole new model. As a vampire slayer she might have been another symbol of repression, but she's the sexiest woman on the show. She's also in love with a seductive male vampire, but she is pointedly not under his power. She's the perfect symbol of a girl taking power over sexuality not by bottling it up . . . but by facing it, loving it, and then outsmarting it.—156–57

Have we, as a society, triumphed over stereotypes and prejudices? Or have we merely updated them into modern and equally unrealistic models? Is it a positive thing that women in popular culture are now allowed to be as violent and sadistic as men are? Or would it not be preferable for men to become kinder and gentler instead?

Perhaps in the "real world" these questions would and should be more troubling. In the end, it seems to come down to what the ultimate goals of a society are. Should we be training women to serve in combat in the military—or training men to build housing for the homeless? Questions like this are part of endless debate, answerable by the needs of the times. They go to the very root of how we live our lives, how we structure our societies, how we rear our children. Popular culture is by definition made up of the stories and myths with which most people in a society are familiar. In the sense that every piece of fiction has an agenda—even if that agenda is that the status quo is good—then every piece of fiction has a propaganda element. The most powerful popular culture material has the ability to introduce and make understandable the issues of the day for its consumers. Ideally, a balanced work of fiction lays out different options for societal stability or change, and leaves those who experience the work with the ability to choose among the options or even to invent their own. Whether a work of fiction reflects or shapes the debate over values in a society, is an unanswerable question. To say it does both is to state the obvious and the profound.

On the topic of gender issues in superhero fiction, it seems that, in the action-adventure fantasy world parity between the sexes is a good thing. Whereas this is fantasy serving the forces of commerce, the forces of commerce in return serve the forces of fantasy. People would not pay to read and see the tales of these fictional heroes if the lessons—explicit and implicit—of the fictions did not feed their psyches and their souls. Superman may be from Krypton—but he comes from something within each of us. The same is true of Wonder Woman, Xena, and Buffy. Each generation makes the fictional heroes it needs. What should inspire—or terrify—us are not the hero's powers or gender, but what the heroes represent about our needs, our fears, and our attitudes.

At last, women now have cultural "permission" to be angry and violent without having to be evil. It took several generations of modern popular culture to arrive here. Our society is at a place in history where young girls don't have to hesitate to fulfill their dreams and ambitions. Or, at least, they don't have to hesitate any more than young boys do. Girls' and boys', men's and women's, human potential is seen as equal, at least in the ideal view. Putting this newfound freedom into practice is still fraught with perils both self-created and outside-world inflicted. No one can guarantee anyone anything beyond the Constitutionally mandated opportunity for "life, liberty and the pursuit of happiness." Whatever the solutions to our society's problems—whatever the amorphous definition of "problems" is—the fact that, in our popular culture, men and women can face them as equals seems as important as the fact that women and men today face them together in government and in business. As in government and business, there's still a long way to go. And as always, popular culture in general, and the superheroes in particular, will simultaneously lead and follow.

6

Thermonuclear Families

The Justice League, the X-Men, and the Fantastic Four

. . . I would create a team of superheroes if that was what the market-place required. But it would be a team such as comicdom had never known . . . the characters would be the kind of characters I could personally relate to; they'd be flesh and blood, they'd have their faults and foibles, they'd be fallible and feisty, and—most important of all . . . they'd still have feet of clay.

Stan Lee on the creation of the Fantastic Four
in *Origins of Marvel Comics*

THE most popular pop culture franchises are those that make the viewer/reader feel special and unique, while simultaneously making him or her feel he or she is part of a mass of people experiencing and enjoying the same phenomenon. One of the most jarring and resonant examples of this is the story line in the movie *Toy Story 2*, where Buzz Lightyear (a sentient action figure—aka a living doll) gets mixed into a toy-store display with hundreds, if not thousands, of identical action figures, and must set himself apart from the others, must establish through word and deed that he is the "real" Buzz Lightyear. The charm of the film is that we believe he is the real Buzz, and are happy when he distinguishes himself as such through his actions. (Of course, everyone who has ever bought an action figure has to, in order to play with it, suspend disbelief and persuade himself or herself that the doll he or she is holding is the "real" character.)

What's the simultaneous appeal and terror of identifying with a mass-produced culture hero? It's the same attraction we feel as humans living in mass societies. We want both to stand out and blend in. We want to be accepted by the group—or various groups—yet still be appreciated for the unique and wonderful individuals we (hope) we are. Phrased another way, we wish to be both orphans and members of a family, because we each have individual as well as group needs. We need to be lone gunslingers, and we also need to belong to the Lone Gunslingers Club and to hear the gossip about all the other lone gunslingers. One way or another, it seems, we're simultaneously running from and running toward various incarnations and reimaginings of family units.

If the orphan's mixed blessing of abandonment and freedom is the expression of a common societal fear as articulated through the superhero myths, then the logical holy grail is the family. And the paradox of the family is that we simultaneously try to cling to and escape family structure and have no choice but to create it anew again and again in our lives, including in our fantasy lives.

In the workplace, in communities, in places of worship, in clubs, in fandom, and of course in choosing spouses and rearing our own children, we look to create situations where we are surrounded by like-minded, sympathetic others, people who may or may not be blood relations, but are certainly affinity-related.

The popularity of most pop culture franchise properties is that repeatability of an enjoyable experience, the ability to return to the place where, as the theme song to the old TV show *Cheers* goes, "everybody knows your name." Certainly, that's a lot of what people go to pop culture franchises over and over for. Not only the repeatability of the story structure—the mystery usually isn't "will the hero win?" but "how will he or she overcome the seemingly unbeatable odds this time, and will there be some advancement or seeming advancement in the life of the hero, the villain, or those the hero holds dear?" But the very fact that there is such attention paid to the lives of these fictional characters means that we truly do come to care about what happens to them. In serial fiction, we get what we cannot get in single-event stories. When one finishes reading a book or seeing a film, if it's been effective, we often wonder: "Gee, what's happened to those characters? Did they indeed live happily ever after?" If a one-off piece, we don't know. We can guess, we can debate with our friends, but we don't truly know. In serial fiction, we know what happens next. The commercial success of such enterprises depends on our knowing. But there is a trade-off.

Certainly, one of the most satisfying aspects of fiction is that the reader gets to observe as characters grow and change. But if there is a commitment to revisiting the same characters on a regular basis, then how much change can there really be? If Superman grows old or tired or cynical or fearful for more than a single story line, then the initial appeal of the character is no longer intact. If Spider-Man gets over his careless mistake of letting the burglar go, is there any longer a reason for him to fight crime, or to trip himself up on a personal life basis? It is only in finite timeline fiction that characters really can grow—better or worse, smarter or stupider, sadder or happier. But serial characters—of which superheroes are a prime branch—are forced to stay much the same, year after year, with changes either being incremental and unnoticeable (unless one experiences years' worth at a time and then can see the changes brought about by the evolution of culture and society)—or change can come about by editorial mandate of some kind. The most extreme example of this was in the case of a superhero character published by Archie Comics, *The Fly*. Created by Joe Simon and Jack Kirby—who also co-created Captain America and many other classic characters—the Fly was Tommy Troy, an orphan of course, who discovered a magic ring that opened into another dimension, the rulers of which bequeathed flylike powers to the boy. (Somehow, the image of fly-powers never caught on the way spider-powers later would.)

At some juncture, it must have been decided something wasn't working about the character and the fictional universe he inhabited. Because, in the very next issue of *The Fly*, Tommy Troy, orphan, became Thomas Troy, attorney at law, an adult. No mention was made of how and why the changes came about—and he still was the Fly in his other identity—but nonetheless, there they were.

Most fictional revamps come about in less jarring manners. The most common way to ease a viewership or readership into such transformations is simply to let time pass between one incarnation and another of the franchise character in question. There was a gap of a number of years between each of the film versions of James Bond, for instance. Even with the gap, it's still something of a shock to have Sean Connery replaced by Roger Moore, who was in turn replaced by Timothy Dalton, who yielded, most recently, to Pierce Brosnan. Since Bond is perhaps the only live-action franchise character who has continually and regularly been appearing in new episodes, this is a necessary manner of evolution of the franchise.

Marvel's Ultimate line does the same thing in a different way. The "mainstream" *Spider-Man* comic—the one that began in 1963—still comes out, uninterrupted in its flow. But the *Ultimate Spider-Man*—dealing in the same mythos, but with a now younger and more modern version of Peter Parker—is on the comics racks at the same time.

More importantly, and more relevant to the subject of this book, is the fact that the film and animated versions of Spider-Man hew to the *classic* version of the character—more in line with the Ultimate view—that the wider pop culture consuming audience has always thought of as what Spider-Man was, is, and will be. The way one always thinks of Orphan Annie as the eternal blank-eyed little girl, so, to the general audience, Spider-Man is always 15-year-old Peter Parker. To attend a sequel to the 2002 hit *Spider-Man* movie and find he was suddenly an adult practicing law would be a violation of the compact between audience and storytellers.

It would be like a rift in a family.

Which is, again, a big part of why we find the serial superheroes so appealing. They *are* like family to us. And they're even like family to themselves. But, if these high-powered orphans are searching for a family, what kind of family will they find? What kinds of families do we, the voyeurs into their joys and sorrows, their triumphs and defeats, want to see them belong to? As has always been true, but never more so than today, the concept of "family" has many and varied definitions. And in the superhero world, these concepts of family, as in the rest of the elements of superhero mythology, both reflect and inspire the families that we ourselves wish we could belong to and/or wish we could escape.

Is your family the X-Men or the Brotherhood of Evil Mutants? The Fantastic Four or the Justice League? Buffy's coterie, or the "Scooby Gang" that inspired them? And what of possibly the most popular super-team in current popular culture, Harry Potter and his circle of friends?

There are central metaphors for how we organize our social lives. There is our immediate family. There is our extended family of aunts, uncles, and cousins of various levels. There are our friends, who—from our earliest years—we classify into various concentric rings—best friend(s), close friends, casual friends, work friends. (This speaks to the popularity of the long-running hit TV series *Friends,* some of whose characters are actually related by blood or marriage.) There are acquaintances of various levels. And there are adversaries or in extreme cases enemies, both characterized by hostility, but hostility that differs in level and rationale. (Surely there is a difference between those who do one harm merely to advance their own aims, whereas there is a whole other degree of animosity when gratuitous cruelty is inflicted.)

Even those who choose solitary lives cannot help but have those lives informed by their relationships with others. As the Leonard Cohen song "Sisters of Mercy" phrases it: "You who must leave everything that you cannot control— / It begins with your family but soon it comes round to your soul— / I know where you're going, I think I can see how you're pinned. / When you're not feeling holy your emptiness says that you've sinned." The nature of human life is defined by the presence or absence of relationships with others. The fact that other people have needs and desires as we do, the fact that they are not machines we can "program" as we would a computer—the fact that *we are each the stars of our own movie* (Kerouac), the central figure in our view of the sweep of existence—means that, however well-intended we may be, we have to adjust to and compromise with others. At home, at school, at work, life is about relating to others.

From that premise, that reality, comes the popularity of ensemble works of serial fiction. And the superhero genre is rich with metaphors and parallels that help us recognize and make sense of much of what goes on in our lives. If one of the purposes of fiction is to portray an ordered and logical representation of the events of human life, both on minute personal as well as massive world-reaching levels, then how we prefer to tint and angle our fictional window into these realms is telling.

There is a difference, it is important to note, between *teams* and *supporting casts*. As a rule of thumb, we can say teams are composed of individuals banded together with the purpose of combining their powers and abilities, usually against a threat that is too great for any one of them to handle on their own. Supporting casts can be defined as regular members of an ensemble cast who are important in the life of the hero or heroes but whose primary purpose is not to share in the battles and overt challenges that face the superheroes themselves. In a case like *Buffy*, many, but not all, members of the supporting cast are also part of her team. This is a relatively rare instance. Usually, supporting cast is defined as spouses, friends, police, or military members who help the heroes in various ways but are not part of the primary story lines of a given episode or adventure. Lois Lane is supporting cast to Superman. Wonder Woman is his *teammate* in the Justice League.

The Justice League of America is the most well known of the meritocracy of superhuman groupings. It's the Phi Beta Kappa society of superhero organizations. Superman is a member, as are Batman and Wonder Woman. In the DC Comics pantheon, one can go no higher. These are the ones who set the standard. There are other members, of course—Martian Manhunter, Green Lantern, Hawkgirl, and more—and they, too, are high class, but mostly by association. Their level of achievement and respect is actually higher because they are in the group that you only belong to if you're asked. And you're asked not because your uncle made a big contribution to the JLA scholarship fund, but because you are deemed by the other members of the team to be the best. The Justice League is the most elite and exclusive of the superteams. Even Marvel's Avengers—founded on a similar premise—the fictional result of the real-world commercial desire to gather a company's most popular heroes into one magazine or animated series—were from the beginning more "street" than the Justice League. The Avengers happened upon each other and decided that it would be good for the world were they to band together. And, being carved from the stone of the other Marvel characters, the Avengers from the beginning were bickering and splitting up, changing lineups as often as they changed their underwear, allowing wanted villains to become members—in other words were acting like another kind of family. The Avengers were the dysfunctional family, the Ozzy Osbournes of the block, as opposed to the Justice League, who are more the Ozzie *Nelsons* (of *Ozzie and Harriet*) of the community, the straight-laced respectable family, the one that keeps all its bickering in the basement.

So, depending on your own background and fantasies of life, you may or may not find the Justice League appealing. As opposed to the Avengers—whose very name states they want to get back at somebody—or everybody—for something—or everything—the League is not after vengeance. They pursue justice. Like the DC pantheon in general, they are cool, rational, levelheaded professionals. In the work world, they would be high-powered corporate lawyers, selective and secretive about how they choose their partners. The Avengers would be a Legal Aid firm, or maybe even a ragtag group of enthusiastic but undisciplined assistant DA's, prosecuting people for whom they may actually have much sympathy. After all, there but for the grace of God would go many of them.

The Justice League is the judgmental family unit. The *Judgmental* League, one might say. They have the contradictory metaphorical distinction of juggling family and fraternity metaphors. After all, unless every member of a family is adopted—and adopted as older children— (and that might well be a perfect fantasy for those whose simultaneous fantasy is to, indeed be adopted *and* an orphan)—then a family cannot be a meritocracy. Yet, many are run that way, to the advantage of those in the family unit more willing and able to fit in and "succeed," however a given family defines success. The moment a parent, in a moment of frustration and anger, says the words, "Why can't you be more like your brother?" the stage is set for family as meritocracy. The moment one sibling starts earning more than another, or more than his or her parents, the seeds are sown for the family as meritocracy. Although, to paraphrase Robert Frost, family (or home) is where they have to take you in, we should remember that the quote is not, "where they have to take you in and make you feel good about yourself."

The part of us that wants to be a member of the club because of achievement and realized good intent is the part of us that wants to be members of the Justice League. We want the respect and the moral authority such a membership would bestow upon us. For those who see themselves as truly better and more accomplished—and for those aspire or fantasize about such a state of being—the existence of such a family-metaphor group is inspiring and reassuring. Indeed, we'd all like to succeed based on our innate talent and our brilliant honing and usage of those talents to ensure that success.

But not everyone wants to or can join such a club, can be a member of such a fraternity, of such a family.

In the case of the X-Men, a major part of the appeal lies in the fact that the team's members are brought together by an agency and by forces outside of them. They are brought together by Professor X because they are mutants, humans gifted with at least one power or ability beyond that of "normal" people. Conversely, in the universe of the X-Men, people resent and hate those granted mutant powers at birth. That the public in that fictional universe is so refined in their perception that they can tell superhumans with mutant powers from ones with

radiation, or otherwise-granted, powers is an interesting and somewhat lacking-in-credibility aspect of the mythos, but it is accepted in
the same way that we can accept people have such powers in the first
place. Again, it is an unforeseen, or at best discounted, consequence of
the entire X-Men premise and franchise lasting so long past its initial introduction some four decades ago.

As Richard Reynolds notes in *Super Heroes, a Modern Mythology,*

> . . . the whole theme of the X-Men—the isolation of mutants and their alien-
> ation from "normal" society—can be read as a parable of the alienation of
> any minority . . . of a minority grouping determined to force its own place
> within society.—79

Much as members of the same racial or ethnic group may find themselves lumped with and forced into common cause with others who
may have no other connection to them besides the commonalties of
chance, so mutants find themselves pushed into social units with those
with whom they have nothing in common except the Cain-like mark of
the mutant, sometimes visible, sometimes not.

(In Marvel's 1980s *Firestar* limited series, writer Tom DeFalco posits
that there is indeed a "mark of the mutant," an M-shaped series of lines
on a person's palm that would indicate mutantcy. Of course, almost
every person has lines on their palms that could be interpreted as looking similar to an *M*. The idea is that we all want to be part of the romantic notion of mutants as outcasts. Mutantcy would make us special
and different, able therefore, in some part of our minds, to feel that any
adversity we encounter in life is because we are mutants—daring, out-
cast rebels, who—like all superheroes—and unlike all supervillains—
use our power with restraint, charitably choosing not to destroy the
unthinking person who wishes to do us physical or psychic harm. "If
they only knew. . . .")

The X-Men, then, are in some ways most like the real family situations into which people find themselves thrust. There is no meritocracy,
no choice, no passing a test or showing a record of achievement. There
is just, somehow or other, "showing up." The appeal here is analogous
to that of the solo Spider-Man. No need to be from another planet
(though Superman does have at the very least that in common with
other Kryptonian survivors), no need to train yourself like Batman to
the peak of human abilities. No, you just have to be born with an "X"-tra
ability, preferably one that's more exciting than being able to wiggle
your ears really fast. Just as Spider-Man only had to be bitten by the spider, so mutants—"good" and "evil" alike—have to be born with their
abilities. The person across from you on the bus could be one. Your
teacher could be one.

You could be one.

And when you're freak, you need a family of freaks. Not the family
whose genetic mutations made you into a freak—not the family you
were born into. You need a surrogate family, one composed of those the
world has abused and persecuted the way you have been all your life.
Especially in adolescence, the romantic notion of belonging to a persecuted minority—whether or not one really is—has great appeal. Certainly, it is the rationalization for much antisocial behavior from time
immemorial. "Somebody did something bad to me, and so I will do it
back to them." From the schoolyard to the mass graveyards of despots
and genocidal conquerors, this is at bottom the fuel that fires the emo-
tion and hence the action. That these actions usually don't solve problems or undo the damage—real or imagined—that had been inflicted
doesn't change this underlying need for payback that seems ingrained
in humans.

No wonder, then, that the plight of the mutants is so universally
compelling. If all the world's a stage, then among the parts we play at

different times are both persecutor and persecuted. In less dramatic ways than real-life dictators and their victims as well as fictional villains and the targets of their rage and hate, we daily are the dispensers and recipients of injustice. A sadistic boss plays on our worst fears and doubts. But then, the victim of that abuse may shout a torrent of obscenities at an undeserving bus driver on the way home. The cycle continues, until you get home to the bosom of your loving family—here your wife will tell you that you've failed, yet again, to do your share of the housework and childcare duties. And your children, when you attempt to relate to them, will tell you that they wish the parents down the block were their parents.

But—isn't your family where you take solace and shelter? Sometimes. One hopes, most of the time. But even families that get along well have their share of strife and conflict. Comes with the territory. You're related. You have to stay together, at least until you can be emancipated, and make the most of the situation since fate has decreed that you are a unit, a family. And while those bonds can be torn asunder, more commonly they are not, and if they are, they are replaced by some other family situation where there is no guarantee you'll fare any better.

The mutant fantasy allows you some escape from this. Xavier's X-Men—and to a degree their evil counterparts, the Brotherhood, led by Magneto—are thrust together, like a family, by a fate that doesn't care if they like being together or not. Where the mutant family differs from the everyday family, is that their very being together is the result of and in service to a higher purpose. Is it a purpose the "family" members would choose in the best of all possible worlds? No. Is it a romantic one for those reading or viewing the sturm und drang-filled exploits of the X-Men? Of course. It's a fantasy all about finding your *real* family. It's you *and* them against the world. No matter how much you bicker and fight, they're the ones who will protect you, as you will them. For the reader/viewer, it's like the security of being a member of a cult without actually having to join one.

A version of this fantasy that's extremely well known and popular—a TV series which lasted seven seasons until its recent cancellation—is, of course, *Buffy the Vampire Slayer.* Instead of mutantcy, Buffy and her crew are brought together by the existence of a nexus of evil—the Hellmouth—that exists in their hometown, and which only Buffy, one of a line of Slayers who are picked by arcane forces each generation to guard the world from vampiric evils, can effectively fight. But various circumstances dictate that Buffy's supporting cast is also her team.

The team—which includes the Slayer herself, the non-powered but courageous Xander, the wiccan Willow, the werewolf Oz, the former vengeance demon Anya, and Buffy's mentor Giles—form a faux family that, for the sake of the world itself must come and stay together to fight evil. Could Buffy do it alone? Possibly. Does having the team "back her up" (to continue our earlier rock-band analogy) make her more effective? Almost always. Of course, having to plan and compromise with the rest of the team makes Buffy have to do things differently than she might like. But the X-Men-inspired "freaks like us" family substitute metaphor is the overriding one here. It's a fantasy that goes so far, and twists the family metaphor so smartly, that in its last few seasons the series even introduced a previously nonexistent kid sister for Buffy—Dawn—who was added to the characters' lives by the scheming of a villain, but who was kept around, complete with "implanted" memories—which were retroactively real—so that Buffy would have a sister.

This is an inspired riff on the X-Men family-substitute fantasy. Not only do you get to improvise a non-related family for yourself, but you even get to have bestowed on you an *actual* family member created by

magic. (These sorts of twists in the fabric of reality that then have lasting consequences are a staple of superhero-comics storytelling, especially in the X-Men line, where alternate-reality cast members come and
go as if other universes were just really distant stops on the subway.)
Creator Joss Whedon even has the Buffy cast members refer to themselves at times as "the Fantastic Four," (and also, as discussed earlier, as
"the Scooby Gang"), though the series contains many homages and al-
lusions to the X-Men, including referring to Willow-gone-temporarily
evil as "Dark Phoenix," referencing the evil incarnation of X-Man team
member Jean Gray.

The eponymous hero of the *Harry Potter* books and films is another
example of the ubiquity of the team as family. Harry—an orphan with
great power—is unappreciated at home, where he is under the care of
his abusive aunt and uncle. It is only with his recruitment and acceptance by his "real"—which is to say, "self-created" family—that he dis-
covers and accepts who he is. Through leaving the family the world has
shoved him into, he is able to discover the familylike unit he can nur-
ture and be nurtured by.

Of course, once at Hogwarts, the Wizard's Academy, Harry still
must find the correct and fitting group within which to exist. He must
find his own family even within the extended family of the Academy.
When he does find Hermoine and Ron, it is with them that he is most
effective.

The familylike unit that Harry finds is a hybrid, somewhere between
the meritocracy of the Justice League and the "forced together" nature
of the X-Men. Harry could have gone on living the lie that was his life.
But as, essentially, "lost royalty"—his parents having been great, murdered sorcerers—Harry may lean more toward the X-Men mythos,
even though the world he inhabits feels more orderly and tidy than the
X-World and more like the Justice League world. Still, the fact that

Harry's schooling is so structured—unlike the X-Men's, who, though students at Xavier's Academy never seem to actually attend class—gives a reader or viewer the sense that Harry and his friends are held to standards that are quantifiable and measurable. And that would be the very definition of a meritocracy. We can look at Harry Potter as X-Men lite, perhaps, which is perfectly appropriate for a franchise aimed at younger children.

Looking to another corner of popular culture, one could even posit that the X-Men version of the desire for self-created family has something in common with being a member of comics (and other types of) fandom. Comics fans, especially in recent years, see themselves as members of a threatened affinity group. The decrease in comics sales, ironically (a word comics people love to use) coincidental with heightened profit-generating public awareness of, and affection for, superheroes, via movies and TV series, only makes fans feel more "persecuted" and more avant garde for their specialized tastes in pop culture. Fandom, with its clubby, exclusionary aura, knew before the general public that "superheroes are cool." But fans were ostracized by their peers for liking stuff allegedly aimed at kids or "geeks." Comics came to be the preserve, in recent years, of hardcore readers and collectors, and the same clubbiness—the familylike sensibility—that attracted fans also tended to alienate casual readers. In some perverse sense, comics fans—embracing the pejorative "geek" designation became the mutants of their own world, feared and hated (or perhaps condescended to and avoided) by a humanity that they wish would simply leave them alone. At least this could be one interpretation of the grandiose self-image of many fans, bemoaning the dwindling of their beloved entertainment hobby—now obsession more than mere pastime—but secretly reveling in the almost custom-made products they feel the need to trash anonymously in online chat rooms.

Although needing to expand beyond this dwindling audience to survive and grow, the comics companies, paradoxically, also need to serve the fan community, since the members of that circle are the only "sure things" in terms of comic-magazine purchasers. The fact that so many comics creators are from the ranks of fandom means that, while much of their work is filled with passion, it is passion that can generally only be appreciated by fellow fans, and so, despite lip service paid to the desire to expand markets, many comics produced at present serve that club—that family—of other aficionados, or fanatics, as the case may be.

Comics fandom is not so much out of touch with the interests of the broader audience—the popularity of recent superhero movies such as *X-Men, Spider-Man, Blade, Daredevil,* and the *Harry Potter* films, and of TV shows such as *Smallville* and *Buffy* attest to that—as it is eager to somehow set itself above the "common" lovers of such material onto another level of "special" appreciation. In its way, this is the highest expression of love for the source material, but it is a love that is often smothering and obsessive. Perhaps, for some members of fandom, it is a reaction to and/or a reenactment of their own family lives—a perfect cocoon of like-minded people, unrelated by birth. There are hints of the meritocracy of the Justice League as well as of the romantic notion of being persecuted by society that is found in the X-Men paradigm. There is very little, one might say, of the third family metaphor, which we shall now explore.

This third family archetype in superhero media is exemplified by the Fantastic Four. This is the family least removed by metaphor from an actual family. The FF was justly famous as the first truly modern superhero team—indeed, as the first of the modern Marvel superheroes. The team has the distinction of either getting there first, or paving the way, for many of the firsts claimed by Spider-Man, the Hulk, the Avengers and, of course, the X-Men. The FF can be seen as the Swiss Family Robinson with superpowers. That is, the FF is less perfect than the Justice League, more stable than the Avengers, and more respectable than the X-Men. They're probably like most families: not perfect, but not engaged in extreme internecine conflict on a continual basis, either. They mostly get along, they have some squabbles and fallings out, they sometimes do things that not everyone in the unit wants to do, they have a leader who as often as not needs help.

It is a tribute to the strength of the FF concept, created by Stan Lee and Jack Kirby, that, despite not ever having a major motion picture released (though one is scheduled to be produced soon) and not having a cartoon series in production for decades, the notion of "Fantastic Four" is widespread among those who follow popular culture. The series was created, as Stan Lee tells it, by fiat of his publisher, Martin Goodman, who wanted Marvel to have a series that could compete with the then-very-popular Justice League of America (itself an updating of the 1940s Justice Society of America). This dictate from his boss coincided with Lee's disillusionment with the comic-book industry, in which he had been toiling since his teens, when a temporary job became a career. More than two decades after beginning, Lee, as he famously recounts the tale, was ready to leave the business. He was tired of being a trend-follower, putting out imitations of other companies' comics in a corporate publishing structure in which the comics, though once prominent, were now a footnote.

Lee, at thirty-eight, saw little future for himself in comics, and even less opportunity for self-expression. . . . He was planning to start a new career, but his wife Joan convinced him to go out in a blaze of glory, "She said to me, 'if you're planning to leave anyway, why don't you just turn out a couple of books the way you think they should be done, and get it out of your system before you actually quit?'"

Daniels, *Marvel*—84

The team is held together by bonds of love, loyalty, and commitment. They generally seem to like each other. And the structure of their relationships is very contemporary. Their origin establishes them as an (older) man—Reed Richards—and his fiancée, Susan Storm, who is a good ten to twenty years younger. The two of them and her kid brother Johnny are then joined by Reed's best friend, Ben Grimm, on an adventure into space, the specific goal of which has continually changed over the four decades of the franchise's existence. As the legend goes, Cosmic Rays in space gave them superpowers, with Ben getting the tragedy-inducing side effect of gaining super-grotesqueness along with super strength. Still linked to the traditions of heroes before them, it was taken for granted they would use their powers to fight the good fight. As the Thing says to Reed after the four have discovered their newfound powers: "You don't have to make a speech, big shot! We understand! We've gotta *use* that power to help mankind, right?"

> *. . . this new group of superheroes was like no set of superheroes anyone had ever seen. They had the powers of superheroes, but they didn't act like superheroes. They acted something like monsters—and something like real people.*

Jones and Jacobs, *The Comic Book Heroes*—51

As Jones and Jacobs imply, the Fantastic Four were groundbreaking. In a pop-culture world where the Justice League's fraternal "Are-you-good-enough-to-belong?" mentality defined pretty much all superhero associations, the hybrid family structure of the Fantastic Four, with its foreshadowing of the X-Men's "freaks like us" raison d'être and even of Spider-Man's power-responsibility linkage, was novel. There was no precedent for these imperfect heroes related through both blood and circumstance.

As time passed, one of the revolutionary Marvel contributions to the superhero genre came into play with the FF. The team *did* grow and change in some ways, certainly more than active (as opposed to retired or other-reality-dwelling) superheroes before them were generally allowed to. This is where their modern family nature really comes into play. Reed (Mr. Fantastic) and Sue (the Invisible Girl, later Invisible Woman) did get married, and in the almost overnight, by comics-world terms, span of three years. (Compare that to the 50 or so years it took Superman and Lois Lane to finally get hitched.) Johnny (the Human Torch) was now Reed's brother-in-law. Reed and Sue had a child—the first superhero union to create progeny—not long after, Franklin, who, though slow to age and mature, has had his own share of cosmic adventures, including an incarnation of himself as an all-powerful adult. Reed and Sue have even been through a miscarriage and, more recently, the birth of a baby girl. So the FF are very much a family. Most of them, anyway.

Turning into the monstrous Thing made Ben Grimm the melodramatic center of the series. Despite being "tamed" over the years to make him look more appealing on garments and mugs, the Thing maintains a raging core that threatens the stability of the family, combined with strength both of body and character that is a stabilizing force for the team. Ben is the "beloved uncle" figure, but in a modern, extended-family way that a nonrelated friend of a family's might become an honorary uncle. There is no blood or marital tie. Still, he and the Torch have always had a sibling relationship. They're devoted to each other, play practical jokes on one another, and occasionally inadvertently hurt each other's feelings.

From the beginning, the team has been marked by arguments, snits, various break ups within the group, and members storming out only to come back when dire circumstances require it. Sue and Reed's marriage have endured separations and the temptations of other possible objects of their affections. Different heroes are sometimes added to the team as substitutes or attempted replacements, but the series inevitably returns to the core quartet of family members.

Despite their literally fantastic milieu, the FF is perhaps the most realistic family fantasy unit. Their appeal is not to those whose family fantasies lean toward the meritocracy model. Reed may be a brilliant scientist and Ben was an accomplished pilot, but Sue and Johnny had no real skill sets that would have made them desirable or necessary for an experimental space voyage. They were there because of bonds of love and/or familial relationship. When adversity struck them, the four crash-landed to discover that they had gained great powers, although the Thing had been cursed with his grotesque appearance, which led from the beginning to anger and resentment on his part against Reed as well as Reed's relatives. But through the crucible of this "family" group's inner tensions comes the strength of their ties. Like a real family, they do not claim to be perfect or without strife. But there seems to be enough in the setup for each of them to feel it is worthwhile to stay together.

This may be the very reason it has taken so long for this status quo shattering superhero concept to find form in memorable film or television incarnations. Although the X-Men, the Justice League, and superhero-themed series such as Buffy and Harry Potter have all had periods of being considered phenomena in the wider culture, the Fantastic Four has not. Neither as aloof and regal in bearing as the Justice League, nor as ragtag and extreme as the X-Men (for whom the Fantastic Four arguably paved the way), the FF are the family down the block, neither perfect enough to be role models, nor extreme enough in their neuroses to be romantically tragic but, nonetheless, all too human in their super-humanity.

Still, standing astride this middle ground may be why, despite their being confined to comics and a couple of simplistic cartoon series, the team is well known to the public in a way that, say Daredevil, who had a recent successful movie, or Steel, who had a forgettable film in the 1990s, are not. The FF changed the way we look at superheroes and the way we use them as metaphors for family life. They impacted popular culture in profound and wide-reaching ways. In that mysterious manner that pop culture and its effects are disseminated in ways removed from the more easily understood and charted patterns of publicity and advertising, in some near-mystical route that incorporates but is not limited by "word-of-mouth," the quartet has really become part of mass culture and, to some degree, a lens through which we look at family relationships.

Which family metaphor is closest to "real life?" Which has the most resonance in the popular imagination? At this point in history, it seems the X-Men reflects most recognizably. This comes as no surprise in an era in which values are so fragmented and norms up for grabs. In an era when seemingly no one can decide on the standards for merit, in a time of ad hoc modern families, where parents and siblings come and go with regularity, it makes sense that the familylike unit of people forced together by common problems and afflictions would be the one of which a romanticized version would be the most desirable. We may see ourselves as outcasts and freaks, but none of us want to think of ourselves as being truly, frighteningly, alone.

7

You Wouldn't Like Me When I'm Angry

The Hulk, Judge Dredd, and Wolverine

The Hulk smashed through the walls of fear I'd been carrying inside me and freed me to feel everything I had been repressing: rage and pride and the hunger for power over my own life. . . . He hadn't smashed all my problems, but he'd led me to a new sense of myself.

Gerard Jones, *Killing Monsters*

YOU don't have to be Sigmund Freud to figure out that the fantasy of the superhero involves empowerment. The child imagines he's not just an adult, but an incredibly powerful adult. The adult imagines he can lift trucks and smash through walls. This slow-running kid imagines himself able to break the sound barrier. The set-upon employee imagines he can level the building he works in. The mugging victim imagines pursuing and exacting vengeance on his attacker.

After all, why would you imagine yourself, or identify with, imaginary power-figures if things were OK? If your life and its elements were all perfectly in balance, then your fantasies would be of an

entirely different nature. Maybe they would involve peacefully changing things through kind words and charitable deeds. Maybe they
would involve working for disarmament and international harmony.
You'd focus your energy on "healing the world," as the old Jewish expression (*tikkun olam*) goes.

There are, of course, many who do that. Superman himself, in his
early stories, was a liberal, Rooseveltian do-gooder, battling corrupt
politicians and wife-beaters, going up against forces large and small
that threatened the average citizen in the days of the Great Depression.
Despite having his own problems, being an orphaned alien in a world
not that friendly to either, Superman chose to use his power proactively
to do good on behalf of the downtrodden. One never gets the sense that
Superman is trying to put things in his *own* life back into some kind of
balance. The Superman school of heroes includes many long-lived and
successful characters. They range from the Flash to Green Lantern to
Wonder Woman, even to the X-Men and Spider-Man (though the latter
two, as emblematic of the modern Marvel-style heroes, are more complex cases, as we will discuss later). Interestingly, Batman's sidekick
Robin can be included among these.

In the Superman school of superheroism, there is a vein of gentleness
and civility. Whatever violent acts the Man of Steel commits are committed in a rational and positive manner. He's your friend. Mr. Rogers
in tights. He's had his share of bad breaks, but his life seems so bereft of
the kinds of problems most people face that he has to invent Clark Kent
so he can dabble in everyday life and see just what it is the rest of us are
always whining about. Of course, when you're Superman—or Clark
Kent—a lot of what would be problems for a normal human are not
problems for you. If Superman gets hit by the proverbial bus, it's the
bus's passengers who will be hurt, not the Man of Steel.

But there's that other school of superheroes that is not so sanguine.

They are the ones whose roots are in grievous injustice—real or perceived or both—done to them. These are the heroes whose initial impetus comes from sudden, violent loss or change, or from wellsprings of childhood anger triggered by some traumatic, science-based calamity. These are the heroes, of course, of the Batman school. Besides the traumatized Bruce Wayne, they include Daredevil, the Punisher, Elektra, Wolverine, and, second in significance only to Batman himself, the Incredible Hulk.

> *What makes Batman so different from Superman is that his character is formed by confronting a world that refuses to make sense . . . madness is a part of Batman's special identity, and [his] obsessive character links him with his enemies in a more personal way than, say, Superman.* Reynolds —67

Batman and the other angry costumed characters cloak their rage and bloodlust in all sorts of rationalizations and codes of behavior that they themselves establish. But inside them all is an engine of rage and entitlement. Inside them all is an Incredible Hulk.

The Hulk is the distilled essence of anger, from pouting, shrieking infant to tantrum-throwing four-year-old to insolent adolescent to the adult set upon by corrupt politicians, venal corporations, and out-of-control street crime. The Hulk looks at the world as it is and says—well, he doesn't really say much of anything. He doesn't have to. He's angry. He simultaneously wants to run away and stay and fight. His reaction to the world is several *irreconcilable* reactions—which means he is going to be angry no matter what. And when he's angry, he lashes out with all the power at his command.

Created in 1962 by Marvel's Stan Lee and Jack Kirby, the Hulk was the encore to their Fantastic Four. With a hit on their hands, and noticing that the Frankenstein's Monster character was experiencing one of its periodic resurgences in popularity, Stan Lee decided that the follow-up to the popular foursome would be a monstrous hero. The FF's own Thing character was surprisingly proving the most popular in a group that consisted of a square-jawed hero type, a tousle-headed teen matinee idol figure, and an attractive blond with a Jacqueline Kennedy hairdo. Yet the misanthropic, cynical—and perpetually angry—Thing was proving to be the most appealing character. The Thing was the first superhero who didn't like being one. He acquired great strength, but was also made grotesquely ugly by the same cosmic rays that gave his teammates their super powers. The next logical step, in many ways, was a superhero who was more of a monster than the Thing, who, after all, maintained Ben Grimm's brain, memories, and values. The questions were, first, would an audience feel connection to a monster-hero? And, secondly, what would a monster-hero *be*, anyway?

The classic Universal movie monsters were as much menace as anything else. They were victims, true—even Count Dracula could arguably be said to be the victim of his blood-hunger, of the vampire's curse. (The cult-favorite soap opera *Dark Shadows* would be the first to deal with such a conflicted character.) Certainly the Wolf Man and Creature didn't ask for their tortured existences. But their afflictions made them, willingly or not, dangerous to those around them. And so they were hated, hunted, and all the rest that comes with being a monster. Their power was their curse, and this simultaneously was what made them intensely appealing to audiences.

But one thing they were not, on a consistent basis, was heroic. They each had only one goal. Dracula for blood. The Wolf Man for a cure. Frankenstein's monster to be accepted. Heroism was not on their agenda; doing good was way down on their list. Their existence was their mission. There was no time for such niceties as becoming deputies to the Transylvania police department.

Lee and Kirby had done dozens of monster stories in the pre-superhero Marvel comics of the late 1950s and very early 1960s. Their Fin

Fang Foom, Grotuu, and many others were monsters inspired as much by the science-fiction movies and television shows of the day as by the Universal Studios roster. Lee and Kirby knew monsters. The question was: How do you make a monster into a hero and still maintain the monster's essential element of menace—yet combine that with a personality that an audience would come to love, or at least be fascinated by? And, on top of that, how do you make such a creature a superhero?

The answer turned out to look like it might be combining the legend of Jekyll and Hyde with that of Mary Wollstonecraft Shelley's original *Frankenstein*. The Monster would now have another persona—a literal dual identity—not unlike the Wolf Man himself, actually, but one brought on by the modern twin-edged deity that was science. Bruce Banner was caught in the explosion of a Gamma Bomb, which unleashed—and/or perhaps injected into him—the monster who would come to be called the Hulk.

There was no real precedent for making a monster a hero. We could sympathize with Banner's plight, we could root for him to lose his monstrous side—of course, we'd have very little interest in him if he ever really did—but how could you not root for him? And he was indeed heroic. He saved young Rick Jones from the explosion and took its brunt himself. He was at least *that* noble, even if he did make his career out of designing deadly weapons to begin with—no doubt purely for deterrent purposes.

Every issue of the Hulk—whose initial series lasted a mere six issues—was an attempt to fit the square-peg monster into the round-hole mold of the superhero. The series, while fun and impressive to look at—as prime Lee-Kirby material nearly always was—suffered from that inability to define just *what* a hero-monster was. The concept seemed to change every issue. He was smart. He was dense. He could change back and forth from Banner to the Hulk at will. He was at the mercy of the changes. He fought spies, he fought aliens, he fought the army. He loved humans. He hated humans. He loved being the Hulk. He hated being the Hulk.

One thing stayed the same throughout. He was always *angry*. The object of his anger often shifted, but he was almost always raging, which didn't make all that much sense during the times he was in control of his changes. In the Hulk, you can see the missing link in the evolution of the "reluctant superhero" from the FF's Thing to the perfection of the type that would be Spider-Man just a few months after the Hulk's debut.

The Hulk lost his magazine. But he guest-starred—or more precisely, appeared as a villain—in other Marvel comics. It took that time for the character's creators and his fans to come to terms with the fact that this villain could be seen as a hero. The audience did, slowly but surely, come around. The Hulk became a co-star in *Tales to Astonish* and eventually got his own series again. There never was any consistent answer to whether he was hero or villain. The issue of whether anyone was ever killed or seriously injured during one of his many "rampages" was never addressed. He often did fight supervillains, not infrequently as a member of a team of other heroes, all the while protesting that he hated teams. And somehow, we come to think of him as a superhero.

This was the conceit that fueled his 1970s TV series, a series that lasted five seasons. The very notion of Banner's—and by association, the Hulk's—*good intentions* was enough for most people. He never *set out* to hurt anybody, and we never saw the almost inevitable and logical results of the outbursts of such a mass of power and rage. So the Hulk has become, in popular consciousness, a hero.

The 2003 Ang Lee *Hulk* film had to contend with much the same problem. The film invents menaces for the monster to face, specifically his crazed-but-brilliant father, and takes seeds planted during the 40-year history of the monster to both explain the Hulk's rage and have him take, in an indirect and convoluted way, revenge on the father who experimented on young Bruce and killed Bruce's mother, who died protecting him from that father. In other words, the Gamma event brought out the rage and anger that was in Bruce—and in us all?—that had been put there by the trauma of his father's murder of his own wife.

So, what does all that tell us? The Hulk is in many ways the simplest "superhero" of all. He's strong and he's angry and he smashes stuff. Yet, he's also quite complex. He's angry for a reason, indeed, for a *multiplicity* of reasons. Science has unleashed him, empowered him to express that anger as raw, brute force. It's just lucky for us he usually—and pretty much by chance—uses it to do the right thing.

The Hulk personifies the anger that Batman needs a rationalization for. The "Gamma bomb" in Batman's life was the murder of his parents. Because Bruce Wayne was a rational being, he needs a strong element of rationalization for doing what he does that the Hulk doesn't bother with, indeed, that the Hulk *can't* bother with.

Why, we might ask, is the Hulk, to this day, lumped in with the superheroes? Why was he conceived and shoehorned from the beginning into that mode? Is there *anything* heroic about a raging creature who does good, mostly, because he has been designated a hero by his creators, and that doing good is what a hero does? Well, certainly the character is superhuman. And certainly, he reflects and channels a part of ourselves. Who would not want to give in to, and vividly express, anger and frustration at life's injustices, large and small? You say he needs a plan? A strategy? A goal? That's too hard, too difficult. Rage and destruction are the fantasies the Hulk appeals to.

Let the bastards know you were there.

Who are "the bastards"? Who is the enemy? As with a shrieking baby, the answer is "everybody." When you ask a crying child what is wrong, what is making him or her cry, the answer often is: "I don't know." It's a response frustrating to child and adult alike. It is the existential cry of humankind, the reason even the rich and accomplished suffer angst and depression. Is it biochemical? Is it spiritual? Whatever the reason, something is wrong, something we can't name or define, something that a run in the park or a drink or a visit to a brothel or a house of worship won't cure. It just . . . hurts to be alive.

That's where the primal scream of Hulkdom comes in. At the very least, one can cry out in anger and defiance: *I am here! I hurt! Make it stop!*

One can see how, familiar to us all as this may be, it would be difficult to build a repeatable narrative experience out of. Hence the imposed-narrative structure of the *Hulk* TV series and the fact that the *Hulk* comic probably holds the record for personality changes for one character. The Hulk is the embodiment of anger, the personification of rage—but he's also, like Superman, hard to write. Superman is so powerful and so "perfect" that he must face adversaries who are either unbelievably powerful or annoyingly petty.

The Hulk is so one-dimensional that he must either be fleshed-out emotionally and psychologically—which risks losing the primal essence of the character—or he must be guided like an animal down pathways of heroism so that, in his rage, he ends up doing the right thing. His anger is something others can identify with, but the way he deals with it, after the initial catharsis, is almost always emotionally— and dramatically—extremely hard to pay off with on a consistent basis. Some solutions to the problem over the years have been to make him a Conan-style barbarian, a world-weary Vegas leg-breaker, and, of course, a traditional mission-oriented superhero. To a certain degree, these fixes have been successful, because the character has been continuously published since his 1965 revival. But it was only in the 1970s and again in 2003, with the Ang Lee-directed movie, that there have been attempts to bring the character to wider pop culture audience appreciation. (A 1990s animated series was short-lived and not widely seen.) Again, almost everybody knows what it means to "Hulk out." The phrase refers to letting your rage spill out and become ugly. It's part of our common cultural lexicon, but the character himself—or *it*self—is problematic once we go beyond the initial idea: "Wouldn't it be cool to get angry and smash stuff?"

This is where examining the more focused rage of characters such as Batman, the Punisher, Elektra, Wolverine, Dark Phoenix, Judge Dredd, and even Daredevil becomes useful and relevant. All these characters have an origin- and narrative-based rationale that shapes their anger. It is noteworthy that several of these—Punisher, Elektra, and Dark Phoenix—are considered villains by the world around them, despite the fact that they may headline comics, movies, and/or TV series. Judge Dredd is a semi-satirical character, created as a response to 1970s societal disarray and out-of-control crime, and especially to the overreaction of England at the time to the problem of crime. Daredevil had been a meandering character, his comic going though more- and less-entertaining periods. The character was caught in a revenge-against-crime origin that's somewhere between Batman's and Spider-Man's. It wasn't until the advent of Frank Miller's Will Eisner–influenced writing stints on the character that the concept of Daredevil as a force of directed anger was most effectively utilized. In Miller's hands, the wisecracking Spider-Man/Batman hybrid that had been Daredevil was refocused, so that the aspects of those characters he concentrated on made for an improved, high-octane blend.

The Punisher can be seen as a Hulk with automatic weapons, a response to societal conditions—especially violent street crime, but more generally a "permissive," out-of-control society—similar to those that made possible the elections of conservative politicians such as Margaret Thatcher and Ronald Reagan. The popularity of franchise-movie characters such as Rambo, Dirty Harry, and especially the protagonist of the *Death Wish* films also led to the popularity of the Punisher.

Starting as a figure designed to appeal to the same audience emotions as the Charles Bronson character of *Death Wish* (noted earlier)—a peaceful architect seeking vengeance for the murder of loved ones by killers the courts seemed determined to "understand" and set free—the Punisher had his own violent losses, his own personal Gamma bomb, as it were. Born Frank Castle, the Punisher and his family were caught in the crossfire of a gang war in Central Park. While his wife and children were killed, Castle himself survived. In the wake of his loved ones' grisly demise, Castle declared war on crime—or more specifically, he declared war on *criminals*. No abstract targets for him. He was going to erase crime by killing as many criminals as he could, one by one. The Punisher took this war to a level beyond that of Batman or the other costumed heroes. Although generally viewed as a villain, he as often as not came up against the gentler sensibilities of heroes such as Daredevil and Spider-Man. The Punisher served, as Bronson does, as a stand-in for the reader who is frustrated and frightened by the level of street crime that had come to be common in the inner cities and was played up in the TV and newspaper headlines of the time.

Like Batman, the Punisher saw his loved ones murdered before his eyes. Paradoxically, the child—Bruce Wayne—had the more mature reaction. He would plan and train to eventually make his mark in eradicating crime. Frank Castle, a former soldier and police officer, in some tellings a former student-priest, as well, decided on the much more extreme, fantastical goal of just killing those he judged to be criminals. The Punisher spawned a mini-genre of his own in the print comics. Like Spider-Man and Batman, he carried several monthly titles—oddly, in the *post*-Reagan period, when urban life was perceived as getting safer. Ultimately, as with the Hulk, the Punisher's writers were unable to sustain stories that repeated the same death-to-criminals themes without either a certain sameness or, in some cases, a patent absurdity attaching itself to the character. Even the Bronsons, Eastwoods, and Schwarzeneggers of the silver screen were unable to sustain the popularity of these wish-fulfillment fantasies they embodied. While there is certainly no lack of violence and vigilantism on TV and in films today, there is also no extreme vigilante character of this sort. The 1989 *Punisher* movie was never released theatrically. There's a new one due out later in 2004, as this book goes to press, and it remains to be seen if the pop-culture audiences of the new millennium will sustain such a franchise or if it will seem outdated. Certainly, the concept of a character outraged at the world's injustices and frustrated by the slow progress and "red tape" involved with pursuing justice through established governmental channels has appeal. Perhaps the Hulk's inchoate expressions of rage and frustration are ultimately more satisfying on a global level than the specifics of a character who targets individual criminals or groups of criminals.

Judge Dredd is another character that was unable to make a successful leap from print to screen. He appeared in one movie—played by Sylvester Stallone—which has spawned no sequels or mass-market phenomenon. Created by the British John Wagner and Brian Bolland, Dredd is somewhat more over the top than the Punisher, as much a satire on the angry-vigilante concept as it is an example of it. In Dredd's case, the state of violent-American urban crime has gotten to such an out-of-control point that law is now enforced by "Judges" who respond to crimes, stop them, determine who is responsible, then charge those individuals, judge them, pronounce and execute sentence on the lawbreakers, with the entire process often taking mere minutes. They are empowered even—or especially—to carry out capital punishment. Special Psi-Judges are even empowered—a la P. K. Dick's *Minority Report*—to predict who will commit a crime and administer punishment preemptively.

The reason a readership has continually bought into this concept has much to do with the world that Judge Dredd takes place in, a world that is not merely heading out of control, but is pretty completely *there*, populated by an array of science-fiction punk villains who aim not merely to rape, pillage, and kill, but to do so as gruesomely and randomly as possible. In *Judge Dredd*, the *world* is the monster—the Hulk as externalized, all-pervasive id—and the judges the expression of whatever superego is left in society. The tone of the comics is bleak and cynical, mean and nasty, and—always—larded with humor. It's as if to say, this fictional world is so bleak and horrific, and our own world is so much in danger of becoming this world—that, if we didn't laugh about it, the bleakness would be overwhelming. Judge Dredd may be angry—after all, he is society's anger rationalized, focused and fired at those who would undermine and destroy society—but he is that rage unleashed in a way that he can enjoy almost as much as the mutants, freaks, and everyday muggers enjoy what they do.

As a British-produced comic, *Dredd*, although set in the United States, has a sensibility that is, of course, very much of its country and culture of origin. The speech patterns, for instance, are a British idea of how Americans speak. When translated into an American film with a very familiar star like Stallone, the elements don't mesh as well as one would like. You can't watch *Judge Dredd* without musing on how the role is a long way from *Rocky* and *Rambo* for Stallone to have come, trying to embody the British fantasy of American-dystopian justice. It took an American—the always-innovative Frank Miller—to take the *Dredd* sensibility and infuse it, with his own very significant twists, back into

American superhero language. With his 1986 *Dark Knight Returns*, Miller reinvented the superhero genre yet again, using one of its true icons—Batman, of course—to do the reinventing. The fact that *Dark Knight* spawned a movement of "dark and gritty" (i.e., the protagonists clench their teeth and kill people) superhero comics—exemplified, not incidentally, by *The Punisher*—that missed the point of DKR, can't be blamed on Miller, who was re-energizing the genre. The miniseries redefined even the look and feel of Batman, and was the basis for the *mis en scene* of at least the first of the 1980s-1990s Batman films.

Dark Knight Returns was Miller taking the *noir* elements he had refined in his run as writer and penciler of *Daredevil* (brilliantly supported in both endeavors by Klaus Janson's inks), and mixing in *Judge Dredd*-style dystopic elements to tell the tale of a Gotham City plagued by out-of-control crime, ruled by a simultaneously ineffectual yet near fascistic state. The government's champion is the order-obsessed Reagan-tool Superman, standing in direct contrast to the libertarian Batman, who comes out of retirement to save his city—and his country—from the forces of rigidity and anarchy, which have unwittingly combined to make the life of the Everyman oppressive and terrifying. Much of this happens by the light of TV screens that report the chaos and yet try to assure us all that everything is all right. *DKR* set the stage for the dystopic, surreal action thriller films of the time—*RoboCop* and *Judge Dredd* among them. In *DKR*'s climax, Batman and Superman, after a savage battle, come to an understanding. Though no longer the friends of the *World's Finest Comics* era, they will each fight for humanity in their own way—Superman from within the highly flawed system, Batman very much from without.

Although these subtleties of philosophic difference were left out of 1989's *Batman*, director Tim Burton and production designer Anton Furst were heavily influenced by Miller's dark, frightening worldview.

The Gotham City of the film is Dreddish in feel and look, claustropho-
bic, the kind of place you would need to escape from on the week-
ends—if you could figure out where the highway was, and if
marauding gangs didn't carjack and kill you before you could leave.
Somewhere between *Death Wish*'s New York and *Dredd*'s mid-Atlantic
urban nightmare, Furst's Gotham seemed to be always shown at night,
even when it was day. That a ghoulish Joker would come from the
shadows to shatter your innocence and murder your family seems like
just business as usual.

Why did we embrace this vision of Batman, our favorite anger-chan-
neler? Perhaps because it is a world both familiar and foreign to us, a
bleak foretelling of what could be our urban future. In such a world,
anger would be the most *rational* reaction to the insanity implied in the
spire of every building, in the corruption in every corner of society. So
would confusion. Who is there to be angry *at* when the entire world
seems set on its head? Who to blame—who to rage against? When all is
dark, what does unleashing the darkness within accomplish?

Unless that rage is channeled through a *Dark Knight?*

Like any great character of fiction, Batman has a grand appeal. In his
case, it is that he takes the anger we feel at the world and puts it to con-
structive use. He's not the Hulk, blindly rampaging like a spoiled brat
of a baby, he's not Judge Dredd, an extremist in a world so extreme it
can only be imagined as ours in our maddest deliriums. And Batman's
rage isn't the rage of the Punisher, who is, essentially, a psychotic criminal. The Punisher's moment may come and go—there may be times
when we need a psychotic criminal on our side—but his rage is not
cathartic or benign. He creates a world in some ways more frightening
than that of the world of mutants and killer-punks of Judge Dredd's
universe. The Punisher's world is one with no hope. Things are bad.
They will only get worse if the Punisher doesn't kill a lot of people. (But

also, we somehow feel, even if he does.) And he doesn't even have the pretense of years of training and a judicial structure that legally empowers Dredd.

There are other, more appealing superhero fantasies of channeled anger. There are Daredevil, his lover Elektra, and the mutant (Marvel style, not Dredd style) who embodies enlightened rage: the X-Men's Wolverine.

Daredevil was also the star of a recent popular movie adaptation. Son of a washed-up fighter, Matt Murdock promises his father that he won't make his living with his fists, and so becomes a lawyer. En route to his professional triumph, Matt sees shameful reality—that his father works as a mob enforcer—and minutes later loses his eyesight in a radioactive accident that robs the young man of his vision while wildly enhancing his remaining senses. When his father is then murdered for refusing to throw a fight, the gangster who runs his life has him killed. Using his hypersenses, Matt becomes the crimson-suited Daredevil and tracks the gangster down and punishes him, setting up—seemingly inadvertently—a scenario where the criminal ends up dead by his own machinations.

Jack Murdock was murdered for a discernible reason. The murder was witnessed by Matt as a young adult. Matt's rage was focused and unleashed. Compared to the childhood traumatization of Batman and the sheer randomness of the Punisher's loss, Daredevil has a structure he can hang his anger on. He doesn't have to hate criminals in general or crime as a concept. His rage is directed toward *justice*—in this case, revenge of some kind. After his father's murder was avenged, Matt chose to live the dual life of lawyer, serving the judicial system by day, and costumed superhero, capturing criminals in the act, by night. Of course, the delicate questions posed by the existence of such a vigilante are danced around. If a vigilante arrests you, is that a legal arrest? Can a man or woman who wears a mask in the act of arresting you be considered a credible witness? Can a confession such a vigilante exacts be considered admissible in court? (Such fine points, in a way, make any superhero motivation besides anger almost irrelevant, which is, as noted before, one of the dangers of the modern breed of "realistic" superheroes.)

As incarnated in the 2003 film, Daredevil finds his way from pure anger—behaving more like the Punisher as the film begins—to a more reasoned point of view, tempering his quest with a recognition, as one could reasonably expect from someone who is also a lawyer, that there is a need for justice. Daredevil's quest seems to be more open to definition than Batman's or the Punisher's. It seems to be more about helping out the police and the justice system than assuaging his own inner demons. Daredevil's needs seem less primal, more evolved and mature. Yet there is a part of him clearly informed by anger. It is partly through love that this anger is muted: the love for, and of, Elektra.

Elektra Natchios, the daughter of a man of wealth and power, sees her father killed by an agent of the villainous Kingpin of Crime. Elektra herself becomes powered by rage. But instead of using that anger (and her many acrobatic and martial skills) to fight for some notion of "good" or "justice," she decides to try to kill Daredevil, whom she mistakenly believes to have killed her parent. In the film, her rage is directed first at Murdock, then at the real killer, the truly insane Bullseye. Apparently killed by Bullseye, she is unable to achieve her revenge. She does, however, kindle a tenderness and restraint in Daredevil—a growth in his character, one could say, since, when he does confront the Kingpin, he chooses not to kill the gang boss when he has the chance. Daredevil progresses, in the course of the movie, from the Punisher side of the anger divide to, if not the more benign Spider-Man side, then certainly closer to the Batman zone, which is where he generally exists in the comics continuum. (With the scheduling of an Elektra solo film, we can only assume that her death, as that of so many super-heroes', is temporary. What side of anger she will wind up coming down on is unknown, though in the comics she is known primarily as an assassin-for-hire.)

But perhaps the most interesting of the anger-fueled characters is Wolverine. Created by Len Wein and John Romita, Sr., Wolverine first appeared—appropriately enough—as an adversary of the Hulk. But he soon found himself a member of the newly revived X-Men team in 1974, his adventures chronicled by Wein and artist Dave Cockrum. Wein left the revival early and was replaced by Chris Claremont, whose legendary run on one X-Men title or another continues, after a few years' hiatus, to the present. It is Claremont, Cockrum, and John Byrne's Wolverine (with significant contributions to the legend by Frank Miller and Barry Windsor-Smith) who is the basis for the X-Men movies' portrayal of the character.

Wolverine is many things, and in that may be the truest metaphor for anger in a personality—albeit addressed in an operatically extreme manner—that comics has ever produced. As a mutant, in the way that mutantcy is portrayed in the X-Men Universe, he is a member of a per-secuted minority, *hated and feared by a world he is sworn to protect*, as the slogan goes. He also has only the sparsest memories of his past. This alone can be frustrating and rage-inciting. The images of his past that he can access are full of torture and sadism inflicted on him. He's some-body's victim, certainly, but he doesn't know exactly whose. His back-story involves him being painfully implanted with an indestructible "adamantium" metal skeleton, and sightings of him running naked through snowy woods, howling like a proverbial wild animal.

On the other hand, Wolverine—aka Logan—also has another life in Japan, where he has at times been romantically involved with a Japanese noblewoman. He has also fought the Yakuza and knows much about Japanese culture and matters of honor and disgrace. He is far older than he looks, probably being at least a hundred. His origin was, until recently in the comics, a matter of mystery, and there is still much yet unrevealed.

But, primarily, when fans think of Wolverine, they think of those cool claws he sprouts from his wrists and uses to slice through metal and wood and—especially in *X-Men-2*—through people. Wolverine is the coolest of the angry superheroes. You shoot him, and he instantly heals—and still keeps coming after you, not unlike the Terminator. When Logan is angry, he's as angry as the Hulk himself, and will even occasionally become incoherent, though he's more likely to snarl out Dirty Harry-style wisecracks. He can focus his rage—often referred to as a *berserker fury*—and wade through dozens of enemies. Often, he will end up killing many of them, distinctly marking himself apart from so-called old school heroes such as Superman and Spider-Man, yet still maintaining an audience's sympathy in a way that the Punisher has not yet achieved. The reasons for this can only be guessed at. One reason may simply be that Wolverine is part of a team—indeed, part of an entire persecuted minority. He has the capacity to love and to have, and maintain, friendships as well. Unlike the Hulk and the Punisher, rage is part of who he is, but not the *entirety* of who he is. Again, his goal is not just wailing in anger and frustration, or wiping out an abstract concept. Wolverine's goal is to protect his chosen family substitute unit.

This could well be the key to the sympathy audiences feel for mutants in general and Wolverine in particular. He is not fighting on behalf of phantoms. Wolverine is fighting for every persecuted mutant. And if mutants are seen as the handy metaphor for any and every persecuted subgroup a person could belong to in reality or in fantasy, then Wolverine is the father or the big brother standing outside our house as the marauders advance from all sides with torches and pitchforks—shades of Frankenstein's Monster–Creature and the Wolf Man—who protects us from the evil that surrounds us. If he launches into a rage that he can't control, or if some of those marauders should find themselves on the wrong side of those claws that unknown sadists painfully implanted into his body—then too bad for them. We're sure glad he's on *our* side. The anger has been channeled and has transcended mere petulance and become the salvation of all that is good and well intentioned in us. Wolverine takes our anger and uses it as a weapon, and in so doing purifies us all. He kills for our sins.

And it is good.

8

Changing Voices
From Robin to Spider-Man

Spider-Man was the hero and the teenage helper rolled into one; he was his own sidekick. Marvel's first editor, Joe Simon, theorized that kid companions . . . were important because they gave the hero someone to talk to; Spider-Man talked to himself. In fact, he has delivered more soliloquies than Hamlet.

Les Daniels, *Marvel*

Here was a solo hero [Spider-Man], not a kid sidekick or a team member, who was really a teenager, and a teenager who wasn't happy-go-lucky or goofily cute but truly complex and tormented.

Gerard Jones and Will Jacobs, *The Comic Book Heroes*

IN the beginning was the hero, and the hero was lonely. And the comics gods created for the hero . . . the kid sidekick.

Hmmm. Wouldn't you think those gods would have created the *female* hero to counteract that loneliness?

Discounting for the moment Dr. Wertham's aforementioned contention, in *Seduction of the Innocent*, that kid sidekicks were some sort of gay-brainwashing stratagem, we have to ask: Why a boy sidekick? And why are there so few of them now? Why, for that matter, are there now so few superheroes who are really children? The youngest—including the realistically maturing Harry Potter—are teenagers.

But in the beginning, there were the boys (and a few girls), who had their own titles, who carried their own series, such as the boys of *Boys' Ranch* and the *Boy Commandos*, but these were more the exceptions. And they always had a big brother/father-type mentor figure to keep them in line. The boy sidekicks were there to give the adult heroes someone to talk to and commiserate with. Perhaps they were boys so that, when the conversations stayed on the childish level, as most comic dialogue then did, it would make more sense coming from the mouth of a boy.

And of course, the boy sidekick was a way of making the fantasy world truly removed from the real world of parents and teachers. An adult male and female superhero team would be too much like a kid's parents, or even like a pair of teachers, designing a good-for-you lesson plan. But with a kid and an adult, a youngster could imagine some sort of child-big brother relationship or an idealized relationship with his own Dad.

In the modern era, starting with the baby-boomer pop culture of the 1960s, the appeal of the sidekick was greatly reduced. Robin, Bucky, Speedy and the rest became adolescents. A popular franchise—one that will be appearing in its own animated series—was and is *The Teen Titans*. And the Titans, like the X-Men, are composed of both male and female teenagers.

The ultimate expression of adolescent ascendancy is Spider-Man. Revolutionary in positing a teenager as the central hero of a series—a teenager who nonetheless still feels he has to disguise his youth completely with a full-face mask and to add the suffix "Man" to his chosen public persona—his advent was truly a status-quo-shattering event.

The same is true of the X-Men, who never would have dreamed of using the word "teen" to describe themselves. Indeed, the way they acted and the way they were drawn would have made it hard for anyone to think of them as teenagers. They behaved in such a world-weary and responsible manner, punctuated by occasional horseplay in the same vein as the Fantastic Four's (adult) Thing, many readers thought of them as adults who happened to be in some sort of academy. That they were the same age as the Human Torch or Spider-Man—or even as Superboy and Supergirl, for that matter—was barely noted. They called themselves adults, they were drawn looking like adults, and the audience believed they were.

By the early 1960s, when teenagers were pop stars and movie stars were teenagers, when the unprecedented baby-boomer generation of the postwar period was reaching adolescence, perhaps it was inevitable that some superheroes would become teens. Certainly, the ostensible adultness of the heroes had never stopped them from behaving like preteens, in matters as far-ranging as conflict resolution and romantic relationships. Paradoxically, the introduction of teen heroes was part of the *maturation* of superhero stories and superhero culture. Maybe the fact was, certainly then, whereas children were supposed to be seen and not heard, and when adults were coming out of the 1950s, where the mark of maturity was *repressing* one's feelings, the only age group in society allowed—indeed, *expected*—to show grand emotions was the teenager.

From Dr. Wertham's juvenile delinquents, to Nicholas Ray and James Dean's *Rebel without a Cause*, teenagers were seen as seething cauldrons of hormones and emotions. (Even Archie Comics's Archie, Reggie, Veronica, and Betty were always—albeit in humorous fashion—at the mercy of their emotions. In early 1960s pop culture, Dobie Gillis, of TV's *The Many Loves of Dobie Gillis*, was an open wound of love and jealousy, despite being the headliner of an otherwise lighthearted sitcom.) Yet there was always the realization—and perhaps, the hope— that the juvenile delinquent was just a poseur, a stage, that typical American and Western European adolescents felt they had to go through. The teen mascot of the Justice League, Snapper Carr—and the Hulk's teen sidekick Rick Jones—were fairly obvious homages/knock-offs of the popular Kookie character, played by Ed Byrnes on the TV series *77 Sunset Strip*, who was immortalized in the Top 40 hit "Kookie, Lend Me Your Comb," a reference to the leather-jacketed hipster's constant pompadour-combing. Kookie, Snapper, and Rick were "tamed" teenagers, juvenile delinquents (JDs) without the antisocial agenda. Like Fonzie in the 1950s-inspired *Happy Days*, they took the rage and rebellion of the iconographic juvenile delinquent and made him lovable and charming, all bark and no bite. To the present day, suburban teenagers traverse the malls of America dressed in imitation of the JDs of today—inner city "gangstas"—but when they approach you and ask for the time are often polite and deferential. We love our menacing youth, as long as they're not *too* menacing.

Child-labor laws were part of the creation of a stratum of young people with few obligations beyond school. Postwar America was the first society to have adolescence and its more convivial version, "teenagers," demarcated as a separate group. Up until then, children were children, and often as not, one went to work from eighth grade or so, if not earlier. Young people in their teen years were treated culturally like adults. Although they were no doubt always the same hormone-emotion mixture, they were not treated as a separate group. Especially, they were not advertised and marketed to as a separate group by manufacturers of the accoutrements of youth culture. Indeed, there was no "youth culture," as such.

Perhaps it was the automobile and Rudy Vallee that gave a hint of the adventures, sexual and otherwise, that could be had by young people out of kneepants and not yet changing diapers. Frank Sinatra could be said to be the first full manifestation of a pop-culture icon adored by adolescents—especially teenage girls—but barely tolerated by their parents. By the time the first of the baby boomers were maturing, the US's economic prosperity made it possible for them to stay in school through high school and even college. If these teens did work, it was as often as not for "spending money." There now were teenagers with leisure time and extra money in their pockets and purses. Marketers were quick to realize teens had to spend that money on *something*.

The 1950s suburban sitcom *Leave It to Beaver* featured teenagers, Beaver's brother Wally and Wally's pal Eddie, who were arguably more interesting than The Beav or his parents. Rick and David Nelson of *Ozzie and Harriet* were more interesting than their folks, even though Ozzie Nelson, himself, had been a popular big-band leader. Rick used the show to launch a rock 'n' roll career that lasted for decades, until his untimely death.

If you were born between 1945 and 1955, then by somewhere between 1958 and 1968, there came a point where you would realize that you weren't a kid anymore, but you sure weren't an adult, either. No one was making you work a shift down at the factory. For the first time in history, adolescents had leisure time options on how to use your allowance or your earned "spending money" that no generation had had en masse before, with that freedom now available even to poor and middle-class youth as well as to children of privilege.

So, in a world like that, what did you want from your superheroes?

Well, you probably didn't want to read about a kid sidekick, just the way you no longer wanted to read about the always obedient, crimebusting Hardy Boys the way you once did. You'd outgrown the George Reeves *Superman* TV series with its simplistic views of good and evil, and its embarrassing teen-figure, Jimmy Olsen. You wanted something edgier and more extreme, the four-color equivalent of rock 'n' roll. And if you wanted it, then your kid brother and sister wanted it, too. The last thing a child wants to do is be caught reading "kid stuff." The trick with selling fantasy to children and teenagers is that no one wants to experience entertainment about their own group or younger ones. Everybody wants to see what the *next* stage of life will be like, to have a foretaste of it through the stories they consume. And everyone wants to think that they're reading something that adults think they shouldn't.

This has always been one of the most exciting things about pop culture: *that it is bad for you.* Even if it's good for you—teaches you to read, teaches you values—you wouldn't be caught dead with it if it had a "good for kids" label on it. The most savvy pop-culture marketers have always understood that kids' movies, TV, books, and comics have to be trashy enough that adults will sneer at it, but not so trashy that they will actively keep their kids from consuming it. (This may well be a large part of the marketing problem comic books are up against today. With comics so respectable, they're now found in libraries, bookstores, and even in schools! Where's the forbidden thrill in reading them?)

Robin and his fellow sidekicks had their day. They certainly gave a friendlier face to the grim Batmans and Captain Americas, and indeed gave them someone to talk to, to explain their plans to, someone who could have been the kid reader. The boy sidekicks weren't—ugh—girls, who would just complicate and ruin everything. And the adult heroes sure didn't act like your parents, either. When the heroes went out to have fun—i.e., beat up criminals—they didn't leave the kid with a sitter. They dressed him up in a costume, too, and took him along to join the party. Today, of course, with certain kinds of realism ramping up in superhero stories, it's hard to rationalize why an adult obsessed with preventing harm being done to innocents would take a minor—heck, a kid barely in the double digits—into life-and-death battle on a regular basis. But, as I have shown, the magnifying glass of realism wasn't applied very acutely in the early days of superheroes. Imposing the view of today's society on pop culture of the past would result in a lot of our favorite pop icons never being brought into being. *Sesame Street's* Cookie Monster, for example, is certainly a character with a troubling addictive nature, always vowing not to eat the cookie—and always eating the cookie.

By the 1960s, kids wanted to read less about kids—even kids who got to swing into action at the side of the mentors—and more about what they eventually would become: teenagers. Certainly, Stan Lee had no interest in writing about boys, wondrous ones or otherwise. His distaste for kid sidekicks is well documented. Johnny Storm, the Fantastic Four's Human Torch, was always seen—despite being clearly referred to as a teenager and indulging in adolescent crushes and temper tantrums—as a full member of the team, no less a partner than any adult member of the Justice League. He was entrusted with enormous responsibilities and sent into combat situations where no one, the villains included, regarded him as any less a threat because of his age.

DC's Legion of Super Heroes chose an adult name for themselves, but most of its members had a "Boy" or "Girl," "Lad" or "Lass" suffix to their heronames. They were independently functioning, but always gave the sense of being an after-school club, officially sanctioned by some off-panel principal or the PTA. They were an adult's fantasy of what well-behaved superteenagers would be like.

It took Spider-Man to break the mold of the teen hero, in ways both subtle and obvious. The mythos of the character has become so much a part of pop culture that it's easy to forget just how different he was. So many characters have built upon and outright swiped from Spider-Man, that his shifting of the paradigm of what defines a superhero—teenage or otherwise—is taken for granted, which is always the mark of a sea-change character. It's hard to imagine a time before the Spider-Man "type" became ascendant.

What made him so different?

A lead character who is a teenager? He was the first. A character with doubts? There was the FF, but they had each other to commiserate with and complain to. Spider-Man had . . . Spider-Man. A hero whose first thought was to cash in on his powers, not to use them to help people? A hero who, even after he decided to become a hero, still had to earn money to support his family? A hero who the public thought was a menace and/or a jerk? A hero who didn't fit in with other heroes? If Spidey wasn't the first in all these, he certainly did it better than anybody else did. Spider-Man was truly the "regular guy superhero," yet he did it without trivializing the genre. He could, and did, lampoon it—and that, too, was part of his appeal—but not to the point of destroying it. He wasn't rich or suave. He was selfless, but had a healthy dose of selfishness, too. Spider-Man can be seen as the apex of the superhero genre. Unlike the heroes before him, he is not perfect. Unlike many of the current heroes, he's not part of the movement to "deconstruct" the superhero. Does he have a kinky sex life or like to torture kittens? We don't know. We can conjecture about it, but no one's ever found it necessary to tell us. Still, we know a lot about Peter Parker, and we learn more every time his comic or his cartoons or his movies appear.

Significantly, everything we ever learn about Spider-Man reinforces this key element about the character: we know that, if we got superpowers, we would probably act like Peter Parker. How *he* feels is how *we* would feel. Not eternally chipper like Superman, not obsessed to the point of having no enjoyment of life like Batman, but human in the truest sense of the word. After Spider-Man, there was really, in many ways, nowhere for the superhero to go. This is the character's greatest triumph and greatest dilemma, and it stems from his adolescent origins. This aspect is so important that when it came time to make the Spider-Man movie, he was clearly depicted as a teenager. When Marvel decided to revitalize the franchise, they put out a comic where Spider-Man is again a teenager, while also continuing (for over 500 issues!) the adventures of the version of Peter Parker who debuted in 1962 and has been allowed to age approximately ten years over the real world span of over forty years. Despite the fact that most action-adventure stars are generally in their late twenties/early thirties, the film's producers didn't take that route. They knew that as much as anything, Spider-Man is about coming of age.

Spider-Man is the Bar Mitzvah of the superhero.

As an adolescent, he has aspects of a child and aspects of an adult. These are characteristics that are acceptable—even admirable—in a teenager, but many of which are less attractive in an adult. Paradoxically, the more mature and centered an adult the adolescent may become, the less appealing he or she may be to an audience.

A teenager can hold down a full-time job, but not have any idea of what it means to build a career or rear a family. An adult who does not recognize this is immature or tragic.

A teenager can be unsure which girl he should pick to go steady with. An adult who is tortured this way is less appealing, and more jaded. He or she becomes a character out of *Sex and the City,*

The charm of Spider-Man is that he is *not* jaded. Unlike Batman, certainly unlike the Punisher, his faith in humanity is undiminished. The evil and corruption he sees do not make him despair for humanity. He may go through doubt and insecurity and self-hate. He may wonder why he does what he does, who in the world might care about it, or even if he's causing more harm than good by fighting crime. But, bottom line, *what a teenager brings to the table is knowledge and experience without cynicism and bitterness.*

Contrast this to the cops on series such as *Law and Order* and *NYPD Blue.* Certainly, the popularity of these programs speaks to the relatability of jaded characters. Week after week, the protagonists boldly go into the cesspool of human behavior at its worst. They manage to have civilian lives outside the job, even express tenderness and love, but when inside the work-world, the defensive armor they must put up around themselves is the been-there-done–that school of toughness. To do this work continually, they—and real-life police—must have some inner belief in the perfectibility of humankind. But the appeal of the characters is often their world-weariness, combined with the glimmer of hopefulness that shines through.

Imagine how painful it would be, though, if the cops on these shows were adolescents. The shows would be unwatchable. A teen with that much experience of the darker sides of life—and no doubt they exist—is just too depressing to have as a protagonist of a regular series. This is why adult superheroes fall into two broad schools. Either they are jaded like *Law and Order*'s detectives, or they are wide-eyed and, well, adolescent, in the manner of TV and movie heroes of another era. Peter Gunn and Brett Maverick are pretty chipper—and pretty immature. Even James Bond, at his most adolescently reckless, has a jaded quality that reminds us he is actually an adult, despite the bullet-firing attaché case.

Spider-Man endured an enormous amount of traumatic experience: his parents' deaths while he was a small child, the life-transforming murder of his beloved uncle, on through the endless trials by both supervillains and the civilian life-hurdles of love gone bad, illness and death befalling many of those he loved. But as an adolescent, he never loses hope. Every day, Spider-Man gets out of bed and starts all over again—not like Sisyphus, forever rolling the boulder up the hill, nor like Superman, *throwing* the boulder over the hill with a flick of his wrist, but like we all do, or try to do, when we're teenagers. *Yesterday was tough,* Parker says, *but a couple of nice things happened. Today will probably be tough, too. But maybe a couple more nice things will happen. Maybe more nice things than crappy things. Who knows? Maybe only good things will happen today.*

May as well get out of bed.

Hope fills Spider-Man's world, the hope that only a teenager can have. It's not the inexperienced hope of a child who waits up all night for Santa Claus to come. It's not the desperate hope of the adult, watching the lottery numbers pop up, hoping the ones he or she has chosen will fall into place and change a life. It's the hope that our efforts will probably be for naught, but, by golly, just might succeed. It's the hope that if we keep coming at our problem from a dozen different angles, the problem will be solved out of sheer respect for our dogged refusal to give up.

It's the hope that that there will be someone—a mentor—who will understand what we're going through—and be able to tell us just that little something that will make our dreams come true. It's the hope that we'll find our Obi Won Kenobi, instead of our Darth Vader, our Uncle Ben, not our J. Jonah Jameson. We hope that life is fair, that good will triumph over evil, that the girl or boy of our dreams will see beyond our awkwardness and insecurity to the beautiful inner person we are. It's hope despite the fact that our hopes are dashed on a daily basis. Because sometimes, the hope becomes reality. And that—that one time in a hundred—is enough to keep the adolescent going, to keep him or her coming back day after day.

Marvel's central heroes may have been filled with angst and self-doubt, but they knew that they had an obligation to fight evil and try to right the world's wrongs. These superheroes seemed to learn collectively of this duty through the example of Spider-Man.

After the death of his beloved Uncle Ben, Spider-Man learns that "with great power there must also come—great responsibility." The heroes of the subsequent Marvel comics would learn the same lesson: the powerful have an obligation to help the powerless and battle those who would take advantage of them.

Despite this noble sentiment, Marvel heroism also concerned self-actualization and personal status. Many of its heroes—including, at times, Spider-Man—seemed to have great fun putting on costumes and fighting villains.

Matthew J. Pustz, *Comic Book Culture: Fanboys and*
True Believers, 49–50

Pustz hits on a key element in the appeal of Spider-Man. It's not just that he's neurotic like us, though that does make him someone to whom one can easily relate. It's the overriding message that Spider-Man—and truly, any successful pop culture franchise—conveys:

It's fun to be Spider-Man.

If we didn't believe it was fun, why would we want to share their adventures and imagine being them? And, not only is it fun being Spider-Man, it's definitely more fun than being *you.* But, lucky you—you can join in on the enjoyment, live vicariously through Spider-Man. You can feel the air swish by as he webswings across the city! You can experience the adrenaline rush of combat with Doctor Octopus! We have one advantage over him, though: Spider-Man's defeats, both personal and in battle, are ones we can share without actually having to experience. We can sympathize, we can even learn from his mistakes and misfortunes. It's a win-win situation for the reader or viewer.

As discussed in chapter 4, it's Spider-Man's trademark to crack jokes and have fun while doing his heroic deeds. And what is this trait if not adolescent? The kid who is able to make wisecracks while he and his buddies work off some lunchroom prank with some tedious clean-up assignment embodies the same spirit. Broken home, illness, hurricane, trouble at school with teachers or peers? "Whatever," is the adolescent's response. The adolescent laughs it all off. The ability to come back day after day, and possibly even to learn from the heartbreak and crisis of the day before—that's part of adolescence, as is the magnification of every wrong, every slight, every casual touch or caress into the stuff of melodrama. And, under it all, there's the teenager's need to laugh about it on the bus on the way home from school, on the phone that night, on the Internet in instant message strings that go on and on like elaborate comedy routines.

There is, of course, the dark side to adolescent thought processes and behavior. The shooting spree at Columbine was among the most dramatic, but there are others, enacted in high schools on a daily basis. There is a reason that adolescents are socialized to become adults. As it turns out for most people, even those *without* great power, there must also come great responsibility. To stay adolescent forever is both a dream and a nightmare vision. Spider-Man keeps the possibility alive that every day can be filled with the dizzying highs and abysmal lows of adolescence. No matter our age, we can live a heightened adolescence through him and characters like him.

> *The young, flawed, and brooding antihero [Spider-Man] became the most widely imitated archetype in the superhero genre since the appearance of Superman.*
>
> Bradford W. Wright, *Comic Book Nation: The Transformation of Youth Culture in America,* 212

In modern pop culture, where the sexagenarian Rolling Stones, working with personal trainers to keep their lithe, adolescent figures, draw crowds of all ages, and where Peter Parker's pop-culture "cousin" Harry Potter attracts millions of readers of all ages, it is clear that the adolescent, who came to cultural primacy in the 1950s, is still the fantasy ideal for children, adults, and even adolescents—the latter eager to learn how to do "it" right, whatever "it" may be. The adolescent has permission to screw-up in a way that a child does not. The teenager gets some of the slack that a kid is cut ("Hey, you're just learning.") but some of the melodrama of being an adult ("Hey—you're fifteen—take some responsibility!") Adolescence is like having a learner's permit for living life. You can flunk the road test a couple of times, total the car, maybe even run away from driving for a while, but eventually you'll probably get the hang of it.

The mindset of the most popular pop culture icons is permanently adolescent. The main characters of *Seinfeld* or *Friends*, despite being at least in their thirties, keep on experiencing the agony and ecstasy of being teenagers in adult bodies. Even with the trappings of comedy, the characters have, each year, a more desperate, pathetic edge of arrested development. Pop culture characters such as superheroes, though, can stay adolescent forever without losing their dignity. If Tobey Maguire gets too old to play Spider-Man, someone else will be found who can. The character can remain a teenager forever—or until we, the audience, decide we want them to be something else. For, what is the "hero's journey," if not growing to adulthood from childhood, stopping off in adolescence. And who among us has not been tempted by the desire to stay adolescent, to keep the journey incomplete? Incomplete responsibility in return for limited power has its appeal, at least in fantasy.

The problem with this sort of behavior in real life is that, sad to say, we grow physically older. All options are not forever open. Actions have consequences. People are not objects. All those life lessons are new to adolescents, and an adult who has not learned them is, in real life, thought of as an incomplete—an immature—individual, although, in some regards, an enviable one. After all, if one sets out to make every day an adventure and to continually learn new life lessons, to maintain an open heart and open mind, who are we to judge them? Why *not* stay an adolescent forever? Because it is impossible, of course. The physical and psychological aging process makes it so. We must all grow up in some way or another.

Unless we happen to be ageless superheroes.

This is why, both artistically and commercially, Spider-Man and the X-Men have developed into some of the most successful pop-culture franchises in existence. They are both sagas of adolescents who have the burdens of adulthood forced on them, yet who still maintain a youthful exuberance and sense of wonder. As powerful as are the myths of Superman, Batman, and Wonder Woman (which are about the child projecting ahead to what they might achieve when they're already fully formed adults), they are, in our times, less compelling than the myth of the teen hero, which is about the process of *becoming* that adult.

Becoming is the most exciting part of the journey through life. It's especially exciting since you don't *know* you're becoming until after you've gotten wherever it is you're going. No teenager thinks that adolescence is a *phase*. As teens, we all believe—we *have* to believe—that this is who we are, this is what we do, this is our destiny. Because, not having been adults, we have no way of knowing there is more change ahead. Even if we've "finally become" a dozen different things in the course of a year, we each time feel that we are the butterfly, emerging from the cocoon. That we can personify many butterflies emerging successively from many cocoons is nearly impossible to fathom while one is in the turmoil of adolescence.

Where does the superhero fit in all this? Again, it's with the operatic, metaphorical playing-out of these patterns of growth. The superhero

teenager gets to do it with colorful costumes and to the strains of or-
chestrated music. He or she gets to have lasers shooting from the eyes
or webbing spouting from the wrists, and, certainly, gets to experience
the "if they only knew the truth about me" feeling in a way that is so
important to adolescents. Spider-Man's process of self-discovery is simultaneously about learning strategies for fighting for his life against
Doctor Octopus, as well as the more mundane tasks of finding strategies to get Flash Thompson to stop making fun of him and getting
Mary Jane Watson to notice him as more than just "a good friend."

For many people high school, and perhaps college, is a magical time.
For some it is a pleasurable period, for some a miserable one. It's this giant laboratory where seething adolescents are lumped together to
learn, as much or more about themselves and each other as about the
subjects they are taught. Because of this intensity, we spend the rest of
our lives in some ways trying to relive or trying to escape this phase
usually some combination of the two. The teen superhero represents
these conflicts writ large, colorfully, and dramatically. Through Spider-
Man, the X-Men and the others, we get to stay in the process of becoming. Whether this is to the betterment of the general culture's
development, or whether it makes for a developmentally stuck society
is an important question. The answers to this question determine what
is important to us and how what is important changes over time. They
factor significantly into our decisions about who we choose to represent
and govern us, and about how we treat ourselves, each other, and the
world around us.

It's all about values.

9

Values and Villains
What's at Stake?

THE comics industry spent thirty-five years establishing a set of values—cultural, political, and religious—that pretty much reflected the status quo blandness served up by the rest of popular culture. It's spent the three decades since then trying to reevaluate and reinterpret those values to reflect the diversity of the culture it both reflects and influences.

But does that culture give a &*#@?

Interestingly, the mass-media versions of comics characters that have recently become the very definition of big box-office movies and highly rated TV series have pretty much gone back to the basic, core values espoused by the most elemental versions of the characters. No deconstruction for the movie Spider-Man or Hulk, no wondering if good and evil aren't too black-and-white concepts for young Clark Kent on the WB's *Smallville*.

Not to say that the modern mass-media characterizations aren't deeper, the villains' motivations more laced with Freudian nuance, or that topical issues don't raise their heads. But there is certainly one thing that is never questioned or doubted: that there is a need for superheroes, that someone, who is essentially a good-hearted cop, must always intervene in the domestic and global squabbles that comprise human existence. We can't do it on our own.

Now, any number of comics series—of which *Dark Knight Returns, Watchmen,* and *Powers* are the merest tip of the iceberg—as well as the best of the bunch—have questioned the validity of this assumption. They ask the logical questions:

Why would a sane person put on a costume and take it upon him- or herself to determine who is good, who is evil, and how justice must be meted out?

How could such a person exist without growing jaded and cynical, and without getting killed?

Does might make right—for superheroes and for the rest of us? If not, then what does?

Why would a free society feel it needs such characters?

Why would a free society allow such characters?

The seeds of these manner of stories were planted with Stan Lee's Marvel innovations. Spider-Man himself often wondered about his own motives in doing what he does. From there, it became de rigeur for characters to question their reasons for existing. And this reevaluation was something that needed to be done. As comics readers grew older and more sophisticated, they were ready—whether they realized it or not—to read stories that reassessed the precepts and suppositions of the genre. The problem is, when a mainstream character is involved, there really is no option but for that character to realize that, when push comes to shove, traditional values as enforced by costumed characters unleashing violence on one another is a necessary evil—actually, a necessary *good*—that the superheroes are chosen to carry out. Chosen by whom? None ever declared that "God told me to do it." They attributed the necessity to fate or justice or morality—the latter two being values that the audience was felt to share. But, for whatever reason, all felt the responsibility to do good.

"It ain't a perfect system, but it's the best we've come up with so far," was generally the realization a costumed doubter would make at the end of his or her personal journey of reevaluation. Such was the case, for instance, when Captain America temporarily became a wandering character called, appropriately, *Nomad,* then returned to his red white and blue trappings. He was but the first of many to make such an inner voyage and come back with the same result.

Characters created *expressly* to deconstruct the genre and show us what superheroes would "really" be like if they existed in our world abound today. From *Watchmen* to *Powers,* these series are witty, intelligent, and entertaining as well as quite dark in their points of view. But they're not what the general public thinks of as superheroes. And why would people have such a bleak impression? The average pop-culture afficianado is still faithful to the tropes of good guys/bad guys storytelling found in most action adventure vehicles. They expect those conventions even more with superheroes. The audience for superhero film and TV fare hasn't spent an entire life reading every issue of every comics series, even series starring the high-profile Superman, Spider-Man, and Wonder Woman. They haven't had the chance to get tired of the more simplistic view of heroes and villains. When they outgrew comics—they simply outgrew comics. They didn't decide that they needed the superheroes to grow with them. They left them behind.

Many people have fond memories of hours spent reading the costumed heroes' adventures, but most of those readers haven't been privy to the innumerable permutations and variations on superhero topics and themes that committed comics readers have been. The general public isn't so interested in the topic that they want to spend their lives following the heroes' adventures. They have little or no emotional investment in the heroes growing and changing, maturing and becoming more "real." The way any hobbyist or professional is more conversant in his or her field than a casual observer, so it is with fans of comics superheroes as opposed to the general consumer. The offbeat takes, the revisionist angles, are for the diehard fans, eager for some new thrill, some different vision of their favorite heroes, or of thinly disguised versions of them as seen in series created specifically to deconstruct—and possibly reconstruct—the genre. But even when a filmmaker as offbeat as Tim Burton or as inspired as Ang Lee makes a superhero movie, they know that to make accessible films, they must hark back to the non-ironic, straight-ahead portrayal of these characters.

Today, even "mainstream" superhero comics are veined with deconstruction and revision or, at the least, massive doses of irony. Yet these very elements help keep the medium from a renewal of mass acceptance. It's a tough nut to crack. It's like going to a high-school reunion where everyone expects you to be just a grayer, slightly paunchy version of who you were decades before. You can't do that—why would you want to? People change. No one's exempt from this. Maybe you can even persuade people who came to the reunion to accept and love the new, mature you. You're still you, after all. But—to stretch the analogy to its limits—the people who didn't come to the reunion will always remember the seventeen-year-old you, will never know the person you have become. And most people haven't come to the reunion. They're at home with their yearbooks, For them, you never have to change. More importantly, they want their image of you never to change. You hold a place in their memories that is more important than you probably held when you actually *did* go to school together. The remembered you holds a place in their personal mythologies that the present, real you could never satisfactorily fulfill.

This takes us, in a roundabout way, back to values. The mass market for superhero adventures seems to respond to stories that reverberate the old Superman TV-series "truth, justice, and the American way" themes. Can modern plots and characters be more nuanced and more complex? Of course—they are in all other branches of pop culture. Can they be more violent? Sometimes. It's okay for X-Men's Wolverine to kill, so long as he doesn't do it wantonly. That's part of what he does. It's not okay for Superman or Spider-Man, though. Killing's not what they do.

In their *The Myth of the American Superhero*, Lawrence and Jewett define what they refer to as the "American Monomyth"—the archetypal plot for heroic action stories—as follows:

> *A community in a harmonious paradise is threatened by evil; normal institutions fail to contend with this threat; a selfless superhero emerges to renounce temptations and carry out the redemptive task; aided by fate, his decisive victory restores the community to its paradisiacal condition: the superhero then recedes into obscurity.*

they continue,

> *It [the American Monomyth] secularizes the Judeo-Christian dramas of community redemption that have arisen on American soil, combining elements of the selfless servant who impassively gives his life for others and the zealous crusader who destroys evil . . . Their superhuman abilities reflect a hope for divine, redemptive powers that science has never eradicated from the popular mind.*

further, they ask,

> *. . . why, in a country trumpeting itself as the world's supreme democratic model, do we so often relish depictions of impotent democratic institutions that can be rescued only by extralegal superheroes? Are these stories safety*

valves for the stresses of democracy, or do they represent a yearning for
something other than democracy?—6–8

While Lawrence and Jewett use the term *superhero* to refer to a wide
array of heroic pop culture figures (including costumed superheroes),
their points are relevant and important, despite the fact that the serially
chronicled adventurer does not "recede into obscurity," but rather
stands poised, waiting for the challenge to be presented to them in the
next issue or episode or film, much like a solider or police officer who
fights today and fights again tomorrow.

Richard Reynolds, in *Super Heroes, a Modern Mythology* adds:

> . . . *the normal and everyday enshrines positive values that must be defended*
> *through heroic action—and defended over and over again almost without*
> *respite against an endless battery of menaces determined to remake the world*
> . . . *The superhero has a mission to preserve society, not to re-invent it.—77*

So one can say that the hero's values are the society's values. That's
not to say that the hero is a Republican or Democrat, a Christian or a
Jew. But the rules, both spoken and unspoken, that we live by—the
ones that say, "Our society isn't perfect, but it's pretty damn good," are
the rules on which superheroes agree. Ironically for a group of vigi-
lantes, superheroes generally agree that the laws of the land need to be
upheld. They believe that democracy is the best form of government.
They believe in racial, religious, and gender parity; judge each individual on his or her own merits. In other words, without being overtly ide-
ological, superheroes champion the consensus views of most residents
of Western democracies. They are not in favor of violent revolution to
change political power. They oppose slavery or anything that resem-
bles it. On the other hand, one is unlikely to see them on either side of a
labor dispute, not in costume anyway. They just figure that those offi-

cially sanctioned to enforce society's values could use some help, *even if that help is from powerful, masked figures who operate outside the law!*

We can say that not opposing the status quo is in effect supporting it. More negatively phrased would be Edmund Burke's famous statement: "The only thing necessary for the triumph of evil is for good men to do nothing." This, of course, is where the hero, super or otherwise, is different from most people. The hero *does* something, though it is usually in a reactive way. The superhero is not an active agent of change in society. Once he or she crosses that line, then the mission is different. Then they are not there to protect but to *reform*. And that can be a slippery slope indeed, one that has been explored in comics series such as *Watchmen* and *Squadron Supreme*, as well as in the 1987 movie *Superman IV: The Quest for Peace*. The results in such works are for the most part disastrous. When superheroes try to change society proactively, things almost always end up worse than they were at the beginning.

> *Heroes are generally obliged to defeat at least one supervillain per issue, but the events which lead up to the confrontation are normally initiated by the supervillain. The hero is in this sense passive: he is not called upon to act unless the status quo is threatened by the villain's plans . . . . The superhero at rest may be nursing no unacted desires, and needs only to be summoned like a genie from a bottle in order to redress all moral imbalances.*
>
> Reynolds—50–51

What Reynolds sees as a weakness of the superhero—the reactive nature of the archetype—is, it seems to me, the thing that makes people actually able to relate to such characters. His or her powers and dedication may make a superhero seem like someone with whom we can never feel at home, much as we might admire him or her. It is the simple fact—as alluded to by Lawrence and Jewett—that the superhero, like most people, will not act, will certainly not effect change, unless there is no alternative—that makes him or her much like us. The prospect of no change—as Robert McKee elaborates (as noted) in his book on writing called, appropriately enough, *Story*—must have such unpleasant consequences that a protagonist, responding to outside forces, has no choice *but* to act, to attempt to bring about change.

So the fact that Spider-Man may not act until pushed—or at least until his highly attuned sense of responsibility is triggered—makes him a lot like you and me. A classic superhero has no axes to grind, no agendas to put forth and pursue. The superhero's role is to get the cat out of the tree, not to prune the tree or discipline the cat. The hero's role is akin to that of the idealized police officer in a democratic society.

Villains, however, are indeed proactive. They are never content with the way things are. And they plan to do something about it, whether or not their planned action is legal or generally acceptable.

> *The common outcome, as far as the structure of the plot is concerned, is that the villains are concerned with change and the heroes with the maintenance of the status quo. . . . Superheroes are not called upon to act as the protagonists of individual plots. They function essentially as antagonists, foils for the true star of each story, the villain.*
>
> Reynolds—51

The history of the world, as well as of heroic fiction, shows the above to be true. Supervillains are the dreamers and schemers of the fictional realm. They have agendas, usually involving a new world order with each one of themselves as emperor. Such is the case of Magneto in the *X-Men* comics and films. Magneto, of course, sees himself and his cohorts as being reactive. That is, Magneto is the hero in his own eyes, protecting persecuted mutantkind from the onslaughts of the outside world.

Discussing Marvel's villains, Stan Lee says:

Once we've invented a hero, that's it. He's pretty much the same, issue after issue. He's predictable. And that's only natural, because we've had time to get to know him, to learn to anticipate his reactions. . . . Our villain has to be unique, clever, inventive, and full of fiendish surprises. . . . Most of our Bullpen story conferences are concerned with the selection of the right villain for the right hero, and, most important of all, with ways of making you care about the villain. For, make no mistake about it, you've got to be as interested in the scoundrel as you are in the stalwart in order for the story to work.

—*Bring on the Bad Guys,* prologue

The villains can be seen as having more well-defined values than the heroes. They have a desire to change the world. That change may be out of a need for revenge or a thirst for power, but they are the instruments of change.

As Christopher Vogler observes in *The Writer's Journey:* "A dangerous type of villain is 'the right man,' the person so convinced his cause is just that he will stop at nothing to achieve it" (74).

This "right man" is the most potent category of supervillain. Such characters are inflexibly sure of the correctness of their value system. Although there are heroes who are "right men," they are not so extreme as the villains, precisely because the heroic figure, like the Virginian of Owen Wister, is reactive, not proactive. Even when a character like the Punisher gets his own series or his own movie, it is still pretty clear that this "right man" is a villain, considered a criminal by all right-thinking people, even when we feel or think he may be doing something that needs to be done. (And both the Punisher and Batman may be thought to be "reacting" to the trauma of their origins' violent trigger-events.)

Supervillains are right men. They are so sure of the correctness of their worldview that they have no *choice* but to act on it. Like missionaries of evil, they sow the seeds of their philosophies and obsessions. They *know* what their values are. There is little room for doubt, whatever their philosophies may be. Magneto will make the world safe for mutants. Dr. Doom will bring order to a chaotic world. The Joker will bring chaos to an orderly world. They know they are right—and will not be persuaded otherwise. If this sounds familiar in terms of some current political and religious conflicts—well, they should. The fictional representation of these conflicts is one of the major appeals of superhero fiction. We enjoy seeing the conflicts and crises of our times enacted by characters in capes with superpowers. Seeing conflicts so represented makes them feel more comprehensible and manageable. It makes us feel that there are actual solutions to intractable problems—possibly even solutions without negative consequences. When a superhero solves a problem, it usually stays solved. Of course, the problem may stay solved—but not the *cause* of the problem: the supervillain.

> *The archetype known as the Shadow represents the energy of the dark side, the unexpressed, unrealized, or rejected aspects of something. . . . Shadows can be all the things we don't like about ourselves, all the dark secrets we can't admit, even to ourselves. . . .*
>
> *The negative face of the Shadow in stories is projected onto characters called villains, antagonists, or enemies. Villains and enemies are usually dedicated to the death, destruction, or defeat of the hero.*

Vogler—71

As a proactive agent, a supervillain may become dormant for a while, but he or she—or at least the idea the villain embodies—will not die. This is for two reasons. First, the villain usually personifies an idea so powerful that it cannot be killed. Secondly, the villain embodies the dark side of the hero.

To elaborate on the first reason, one has but to look at the headlines in the newspapers to see the appeal, the power, of ideas of force and violence. They're both seductive and, by their nature, aggressive in their execution. And, as always with human nature, no one really sees himself or herself as the bad guy. Everybody—even when fighting the most apparently venal and self-serving battles—has to see himself or herself as somehow noble. Don Vito Corleone in *The Godfather* is one of the most effective examples of this mindset in pop culture.

In all objective senses, Corleone and his gang are self-serving criminals, masking their venal acts with a patina of nobility and speeches about justice. Yet, we are moved to see them as the heroes of the works, because Mario Puzo and Francis Ford Coppola's scripts bring us inside their minds, making us realize that perhaps we, in similar circumstances, might behave the same way: to embark on a life of crime for somewhat idealistic reasons while seeing that idealism soon corrupted into what is, beneath all the camouflage, doing evil on a routine basis. Since the Corleones are—to again quote Robert McKee—the "center of good" in the *Godfather* universe, we root for them. They are not as bad as the other gangs seem to be, though perhaps if the stories were told from the rival Barzini's or Tataglia's points of view, we might end up rooting for those characters instead, and see the Corleones as "worse."

The Corleones embody an idea that has been around forever, namely that in a world of chaos and every-man-for-himself thinking, people need a strong man—a Godfather—to protect them, *to do what needs to be done, no matter how distasteful, for the common good.* This is exactly what the best supervillains do. Even those apparently devoted to chaos and caprice are exactly that: *devoted.* The supervillain is dedicated to his *idée fixé* in a way that the superhero is usually not. With the notable exception of the proactive Batman and Punisher, most heroes are indeed reactive. "If it ain't broke," they seem to say, "don't fix it." Batman and the Punisher have no problem fixing things because they believe those things will probably end up broken. What makes Batman a hero is the relative restraint he shows compared to the Punisher.

Besides embodying potent ideas, supervillains also often embody the hero's dark side. As in our own lives, the things we detest in others are often those that we fear inside ourselves. In the case of superheroes, the X-Men's Professor Xavier agrees with Magneto that there is enmity between humans and mutants. They violently disagree on the solution to the problem. Spider-Man believes that with great power there must also come great responsibility. Doctor Octopus—who, like the insect that Spider-Man is named for also has eight arms, thereby mirroring (or shadowing) the hero—likewise stands by this axiom. He believes, however, that *his* responsibility is to enrich himself and destroy his enemies. The idea that there is an evil "out there" that needs to be vanquished before it destroys us, whether you agree with the invasion or not, is a powerful one. More than sixty years after the fact, the idea that Hitler should have been stopped at Munich is one of the great what-ifs of modern history. There is general consensus that the Allies should have used Hitler's own tactics of force against him. We should have unleashed our own dark side—which we ultimately did, though it took several years for the provocation to become severe enough.

In confronting supervillains, therefore, superheroes enact our own inner and societal dialectics about issues of life and death. Again, the superheroes both reflect and are reflected by the world that produces them. They are very much the dream life—including the nightmares—of our society.

Moreover, as both "good guys" and "bad guys" are fond of saying, the villains—and the ideas they represent—can afford to lose over and over. The villains, especially given most superheroes' reluctance to kill, can just come back and try again and again. Being naturally less given to mercy, villains only need to win once, and the hero's career—and life—will be over.

Would this also kill the values the hero represents?

Probably not. Though relatively passive protectors of the status quo, the superheroes do represent ideas that are as powerful as those of the villains'. At least that's the hope to which we all cling. We don't want to be relentless crusaders against evil. We just want to go to work and enjoy our time with our friends and families. We will take up arms if need be, but the values our best selves hold to are those of fair play and equality under the law. In hard times, we may embrace our shadow selves, but most people want some version of a fair and just society to be the one they live in.

Perhaps this is why the story of the seeming death of a hero is a popular trope to which the comics, film, and TV versions of the superheroes often return. In such story lines, even if the hero doesn't literally die—only to be resurrected, of course—then he or she comes to a point where there is a need to renounce self-appointed missions and responsibilities. In the Superman and Batman movie franchises, for example, both characters have (temporarily) said, in effect: "This is too much for me. The odds are too great, my deficiencies too profound, for me to continue." But to no one's surprise and everyone's delight, they always come back. Whether a "miraculous" return from seeming death, or a return to the right path, the values they embody are too strong to quell or kill.

We have a need for a champion who will know the right thing to do, the right amount of force that needs to be applied, and who has the resources to muster that force and set right everything that has veered off track. Although, in reality, when mere humans try to do these things the results are often messy and muddled, the superhero ideal exists be-cause we want and need it to on many psychological levels. We need to dream, and superheroes are the embodiment of what C. G. Jung termed the collective unconscious.

What use we make of these dreams when we awaken is up to us.

10

The Future of the Superhero

THE Superhero idea and ideal are ubiquitous. A citizen of a modern industrialized society cannot go a day without being exposed to superhero imagery. From *Sesame Street*'s "Hero Guy" and "Super Grover," to Eminem's music videos "Superman" and the Batman and Robin homaging "Without Me," to the bug-killing "Orkin Man," the concept of superheroes pervades our culture. People who wouldn't think of reading a comic or going to a special-effects-laden superhero film have no choice but to be exposed to superhero culture. The super-hero has become an effective shorthand to convey myriad ideas both commercial and prosocial. When Jerry Siegel and Joe Shuster created Superman, they tumbled onto a metaphor system that everyone in modern society could understand at a glance. So in that sense, super-heroes are with us and will be with us forever. There's no escaping them. The concept is part of our vocabulary for subjects both frivolous and dead serious, intellectual and entertaining.

As far as the cultural moment of mainstream narrative vehicles cen-tered on superheroes, we seem to be at the height of such a time in pop-culture history. The superhero has recently exploded in mass popularity to a degree not seen since the 1940s. The big difference be-tween then and now, of course, is that the superhero of today is best known in movie, TV, and video-game formats. The comic book, where superheroes originated, still exists—the phone-book-like size of the monthly Diamond Comics Distributors catalog attests to this—but it exists for the most part as the pastime of a rarefied audience. The top-selling comics today have sales of about 125,000 copies per issue, compared to the million or more copies an issue of *Superman* sold in the 1940s and the half million per issue in the 1950s. But the permanence of the superhero as an ideal and as a cultural phenomenon is stronger than ever. Each week, a superhero movie or TV series debuts, and another half-dozen are announced as being in production. Although it is inevitable that Hollywood's—and the audience's—infatuation with superheroes may wane, it is equally inevitable that it will, after a period of quiescence, rise again. For over sixty years, superheroes have fascinated us. And from the beginnings of storytelling, tales of beings with superhuman abilities have been among the prime modes of communicating values, ideas, and ideals, as well as excitement. Superheroes have become a permanent part of the pop-culture cycle, like secret agents, private eyes, and time travelers.

Will comics themselves ever again become a medium so pervasive that people will first think of their favorite superhero as being a comic book character? This is unlikely. Too many current cultural factors weigh against it. Still, the comic book has been counted out before and managed to resurge with new ideas, new variations on old ideas, and modified formats. No matter what market and technological forces may bring to bear on content, there is a certain magic in the combination of words and pictures that can only be conveyed in comics panels, a visceral "special effect" that has nothing to do with computer-generated technology and huge production budgets. Superheroes originated in comics, and perhaps they will lead people back to the form.

Again, this may be an unlikely scenario. A more likely one is that superhero stories will eventually become available only as screened products. The conglomerates that control publishing and the other media may decide that supporting comics production as a sort of research-and-development department for new concepts, superhero and otherwise, is not worth the money or the effort.

Probably, the future of comics, superhero and other, will involve a scenario that no one can predict.

But superheroes as metaphors and icons are here to stay. They are part of the DNA of our culture. The superhero will be around for as long as stories are told. Whether these stories will be told in comics, in films, on TV, on computer screens, or via some form of media that hasn't been invented, is the only uncertainty. If some nuclear or ecological disaster should engulf our world, superhero stories will still be told—and will probably be needed more than ever. They would then be communicated orally or delineated with the points of charcoal-tipped sticks on the rubble remaining of our society's edifices. But stories of heroic superbeings—and their villainous counterparts—will always have an audience.

On a more prosaic level, barring such an end-of-the-world scenario—the type of scenario so familiar to superhero fans—the superhero will continue to evolve, probably to diversify and specialize, as our entire entertainment system seems to do. There will be superheroes for all ethnic and racial groups, superheroes of the straight-ahead, square-jawed variety, as well as those who take ironic and satirical views of aspects of society. But it seems safe to say that, just as each generation since the 1930s has had its own new heroes, as well as its own versions of the evergreen heroes, such will continue to be the case for new generations. There may be six Spider-Man movies one decade, then there may be none for a while, then, ten years later, there will be a new flight of them, because some ideas are eternal. Ideas such as:

With great power, there must also come great responsibility.

Criminals are a superstitious, cowardly lot.

You wouldn't like me when I'm angry.

Truth, justice, and the American Way.

These and many other ideas embodied by the superheroes are constants in our society's collective needs and desires, in our very dreams themselves. Superheroes tell us that things will be all right, if we just have faith in our own abilities. With each era, the specifics of how these powerful concepts are depicted and resolved takes on a new character and sensibility. Each generation will redefine the superhero according to its needs.

But one way or another, the superhero is here to stay.

Afterword
Getting Personal

It would be disingenuous for me to claim much objectivity in the creation of *Superman on the Couch*. I have a very personal interest in superheroes, of course—otherwise why would I have undertaken such a work? However, since my life's journey has been both typical and atypical, I thought it would be relevant and of interest to recount some of it here. The trick for me in writing this book has been to take my personal interest, using it to refract my thoughts and research about the topic, and then pulling back to try to untangle the personal from the analytical without losing the passion that I hope drives the book. In other words, to try to explore "What Superheroes Really Tell Us about Ourselves and Our Society," I had to explore "What Superheroes Really Tell Us about Ourselves and Our Society . . . and Danny Fingeroth." Then I had to step back and attempt to universalize my own feelings into those of society at large. It's been an exciting and challenging process.

In the course of my career in comics, I was a writer and editor at Marvel Comics for close to twenty years. As a Marvel staffer and freelancer, I have been involved with the mythologies of all the major (and many minor) characters of that pantheon, from Spider-Man to the X-Men to the Fantastic Four. As editorial director of the Spider-Man line of comics, I oversaw the integrity of—as well as any changes in—the character's mythology. As the lightning rod for "Spidey's" stories, I had firsthand knowledge of what these stories meant to readers of all ages who told us in no uncertain terms what they meant to *them*. I also was the story consultant for the mid-1990s Fox Kids *Spider-Man* animated series, and, through studying and contributing to the "bible"— the official writers' guide for the series—as well as the scripts, themselves, I came to understand what the wider world required of the legend of this archetypal hero, what was important to salvage from (the then-) thirty years of comics continuity and what could be jettisoned. I learned what were the core values of the character to which a mainstream audience would respond. Since most in this audience would, it was assumed, be children, the task of stripping down and rebuilding was especially challenging and enlightening. It was a very educational process.

In addition, as a freelance writer I've written hundreds of superhero comics and animation stories, including tales of Spider-Man, the Fantastic Four, and a "Spider-Man for the 1990s" called Darkhawk, as well as stories of Superman, and adventures of the video-game icon Sonic the Hedgehog, who is also a type of superhero. As much as shepherding other people's stories into being while guarding and minding pop-culture franchises, writing the adventures of iconic characters taught (and teaches) me a great deal about what makes such characters tick, but from a different point of view. It requires me to think a lot about what makes them function, what their appeal is, and then to figure out how I can be true to the characters and what they embody, as well as how to advance the mythology and still fit in some surprises and twists along the way.

Not only have I been the caretaker of superhero icons, I've also created brand-new superheroes from scratch. To do this requires a great deal of thought about, and analysis of, the genre. What makes for a powerful, motivating origin that will resonate through all the hero's adventures? What sort of powers will be appropriate for the times, and maybe even for decades to come? What would be the best costume, whether it's spandex tights or a "non-costume" identifying look? What sort of supporting cast would best reflect the themes of the origin and the series? Significantly, how should a new character be similar to established ones? How should a new character be *different* from those that have gone before? Creating a new character is to immerse oneself in the past, in hopes of creating something new. In all senses of the word it is an education.

Among my current roles, in addition to writing and consulting on comics and television stories, I'm editor-in-chief of *Danny Fingeroth's Write Now! Magazine,* published by TwoMorrows. It focuses on writing for comics, film, and television, with much of the attention being on superhero stories in whatever medium. In effect, one of the main things it's about is what ingredients go into making superhero pop-culture stories that people will want to read, see, buy, and dream about. Through studies of current and classic comics, as well as interviews with, and articles by and about, writers and editors of all eras, I again am required to think about and discuss what makes superhero stories work and not work, what makes them memorable or forgettable, and how the things that people *outside* comics note and remember about superheroes come to be. And, if that's not immersion enough, I also teach comics and graphic novel writing at New York University and other institutions, with much attention paid to superhero stories.

When I started writing *Couch,* I thought of superheroes as a uniquely interesting topic, and the book as one that would have an audience encompassing comics fans, academics, and casual readers interested in pop culture. I first looked at writing this book as something that could and should be done in a cool, professional manner. But the book quickly became very personal. As I wrote about the heroes and their appeal, I was forced to analyze the phenomenon of the superhero through my own experiences.

My entire life has been bound up with comics, as probably can be said for many reading this. If you like or love comics, especially superhero comics, odds are they hooked you pretty young. In my case, I come from a background where the experiences of much of my professional life, and even my social life, have been been played out in the context of a workday environment that is simultaneously a comics—a *superhero comics*—environment. In other words, the triumphs and tragedies (note the melodramatic phrasing) in my career and personal life were always bound up with some superhero saga or other being crafted in my professional life. The potential for crossover between those sides is inevitable. So this topic becomes personal for me in a way that I hadn't really anticipated. I hope that I've successfully unraveled the intertwining threads of the personal and the analytical, but without losing what the personal contributes to the analytical, so as to end up with a richer book that sheds some light on how its readers and the society we live in are affected by superhero imagery and ideas.

In my thinking about superheroes, I went through the same progression that many people do. I loved comics as a kid, dropped them when I became a teenager, and rediscovered them in my twenties, mostly through reissues of Will Eisner's *The Spirit* and the work of pioneers such as Art Spiegelman and Harvey Pekar. None of these people specifically writes superhero comics, though *The Spirit* came close to being one since, among other things, it represents Eisner's commentary on the genre.

In any event, I must have felt fondly enough about comics and my reintroduction to them that, on graduation from college, I applied for and accepted an entry-level assistant-editor position at Marvel Comics.

As noted, unlike many of my peers in the business, I was not someone who kept up with comics continuity through my later high school and my college years. A large part of my first job at Marvel was actually reading and breaking up stories for weekly serial publication in England, thereby educating myself in those stories' structure and in the history of the characters which I had missed in the years that I wasn't reading their adventures.

Once in the business, I read more comics, catching up, becoming more of a fan than I had been for years, maybe more than I had *ever* been. But I now brought a more adult viewpoint to the stories. For whatever reason, there was something about the characters—and about the touchstones of the stories they appeared in—that reached me deeply in a way not unlike the way they had reached me as a child.

People who work in comics tend to look at interpersonal encounters as good versus evil: as melodrama. Whether that's why we gravitate toward superhero comics, or if we enjoy superhero comics because we see life as melodrama is a classic chicken-and-egg problem. Certainly in the age of the Internet, the feuds and alliances, the victories and defeats of comics *creators* are as much narratives that fans follow as they do the stories themselves. As Jack Kerouac exhorted: "be the hero of your own movie." In my case, that movie was—and is—a superhero movie. In a way, I was building up the text for this book without even knowing it.

Finally, writing this book has compelled me to address issues that anyone who makes fiction for a living faces. We transmit values though the work, and we have to assess whether, as part of the onslaught of pop culture, we have, as Spider-Man might say, either responsibility or power stemming from what we create. Are we creating entertainment or life lessons? Do we reflect or create the society around us? I've touched on this topic in the book and it's an important one. I don't know if there's a definitive answer. For most of us, reality and fantasy always overlap a little. When they overlap *more* than a little is where in-sanity begins, I suppose. As I've stated several times in the book, pop-culture both reflects and is reflected by society. Perhaps the flaw is thinking of media and entertainment as separate from our lives. Given the ubiquitous nature of media and fantasy images, there is no longer a clearly defined dividing line between the two. Perhaps what super-heroes really tell us about ourselves and our society is that reality in-forms fantasy, fantasy informs reality, and we have to be careful how we choose our heroes and our values. Sooner or later, realities will con-front us that we, both personally and as a society, will have to deal with on our own, with no superhero there to swoop in to save the day.

We each have to be our own superhero. It's the work of a lifetime.

SELECT BIBLIOGRAPHY

Berger, Arthur Asa. *The Comic Stripped American: What Dick Tracy, Blondie, Daddy Warbucks, and Charlie Brown Tell Us About Ourselves.* Baltimore, MD: Penguin Books, 1973.

Bettelheim, Bruno. *The Uses of Enchantment: The Meaning and Importance of Fairy Tales.* New York: Vintage Books/Random House, 1975, 1976, 1989.

Campbell, Joseph. *The Hero with a Thousand Faces.* Princeton: Princeton University Press, 1949, 1989.

Daniels, Les. *Batman: The Complete History.* San Francisco: Chronicle Books, 1999.

———. *DC Comics: Sixty Years of the World's Greatest Comic Book Heroes.* Boston/New York/Toronto/London: DC Comics/Bullfinch Press/ Little, Brown and Company, 1995.

———. *Marvel: Five Fabulous Decades of the World's Greatest Comics.* New York: Harry N. Abrams, 1995.

———. *Superman, the Complete History: The Life and Times of the Man of Steel.* San Francisco: DC Comics/Chronicle Books, 1998.

———. *Wonder Woman: The Complete History.* San Francisco: Chronicle Books, 2000.

Disch, Thomas M. *The Dreams Our Stuff is Made of: How Science Fiction Conquered the World.* New York/London/Toronto/Sydney/Singapore: Touchstone/Simon and Schuster, 1998.

Dooley, Dennis, and Gary Engle, eds. *Superman at Fifty! The Persistence of a Legend!* Cleveland, OH: Octavia Press, 1987.

Dyson, Anne Haas. *Writing Superheroes: Contemporary Childhood, Popular Culture, and Classroom Literacy.* New York and London: Teachers College Press, 1997.

Evanier, Mark. *Wertham Was Right! Another Collection of POV Columns.* Raleigh, NC: TwoMorrows, 2003.

Feiffer, Jules. *The Great Comic Book Heroes.* New York: The Dial Press, 1965.

Golden, Christopher, and Nancy Holder with Keith R. A. DeCandido. *Buffy the Vampire Slayer: The Watcher's Guide.* New York/London/Toronto/Sydney/Tokyo/Singapore: Pocket Books/Simon and Schuster, 1998.

Inness, Sherrie A. *Tough Girls: Women Warriors and Wonder Women in Popular Culture.* Philadelphia: University of Pennsylvania Press, 1999.

Jones, Gerard. *Killing Monsters: Why Children Need Fantasy, Super Heroes, and Make-Believe Violence.* New York: Basic Books, 2002.

———— and Will Jacobs. *The Comic Book Heroes.* Rocklin, CA: Prima Publishing, 1997.

Jung, Carl G., and M.-L. von Franz, Joseph L. Henderson, Jolande Jacob, Aniela Jaffe, eds. *Man and His Symbols.* New York: Laurel/Dell/Bantam Doubleday Dell Publishing, 1964.

Lawrence, John Shelton, and Robert Jewett. *The Myth of the American Superhero.* Grand Rapids, MI/Cambridge, UK: William B. Eerdmans, 2002.

Lee, Stan. *Origins of Marvel Comics.* New York: Simon and Schuster, 1974.

————. *Son of Origins of Marvel Comics.* Revised Edition. New York: Marvel Comics, 1975, 1997.

————. *Bring on the Bad Guys: Origins of Marvel Villains.* Revised Edition. New York: Marvel Comics, 1998.

May, Rollo. *The Cry for Myth.* New York: Delta/Dell Publishing, 1991.

McAllister, Matthew P., and Edward H. Sewell, Jr., Ian Gordon. *Comics and Ideology.* New York/Washington, DC/Baltimore, MD/Bern/Frankfurt am Main/Berlin/Brussels/Vienna/Oxford: Peter Lang, 2001.

McKee, Robert. *Story: Substance, Structure, Style, and the Principles of Screenwriting*. New York: Regan Books/Harper Collins, 1997.

Nazzaro, Joe. *Writing Science Fiction and Fantasy Television*. London: Titan Books, 2002.

Nyberg, Amy Kiste. *Seal of Approval: The History of the Comics Code*. Jackson, MI: University Press of Mississippi, 1998.

Paley, Vivian Gussin. *Boys & Girls: Superheroes in the Doll Corner*. Chicago and London: The University of Chicago Press, 1984.

Pustz, Matthew J. *Comic Book Culture: Fanboys and True Believers*. Jackson, MI: University Press of Mississippi, 1999.

Reynolds, Richard. *Super Heroes: A Modern Mythology*. Jackson, MI: University Press of Mississippi, 1992.

Robinson, Lillian S. "Looking for Wonder Woman." *ArtForum*, Summer 1989.

———. *Wonderwomen: Feminisms and Superheroes*. New York and London: Routledge, 2004.

Savage, William W. Jr. *Commies, Cowboys, and Jungle Queens: Comic Books and America, 1945–1954*. Hanover and London: Wesleyan University Press/University Press of New England, 1990.

Steinem, Gloria. "Introduction." *Wonder Woman: Featuring Over Five Decades of Great Covers*. New York/London/Paris: Abbeville Press, 1995.

Steranko, James. *The Steranko History of Comics Vol. 1*. Reading, PA: Supergraphics, 1970.

———. *The Steranko History of Comics Vol. 2*. Reading, PA: Supergraphics, 1972.

Vogler, Christopher. *The Writer's Journey: Mythic Structure for Writers*, Second Edition. Studio City, CA: Michael Wiese Productions, 1998.

Wertham, Frederic. *Seduction of the Innocent*. New York: Rinehart and Company, 1954.

Wright, Bradford W. *Comic Book Nation: The Transformation of Youth Culture in America*. Baltimore, MD, and London: Johns Hopkins University Press, 2001.

ACKNOWLEDGMENTS

Many people were instrumental to the existence of *Superman on the Couch*. I'm sure that as soon as the ink dries on the print run I'll remember a few important ones that slipped my mind. Nonetheless, here are some well-deserved thanks.

First, much gratitude and appreciation to my editor, the freewheelin' Evander Lomke, who patiently saw me through the writing of this book. He did just what a great editor is supposed to, namely being there when needed, disappearing when not, and knowing the difference between the two.

Of course, I have to thank all the people who made the superhero stories that have, for a good part of my life, enabled me to revel as a reader and make a living as a writer and editor, and now as a cultural critic. You'd have to put Stan Lee and Jack Kirby at the top of that list, of course, as well as Jerry Siegel, Joe Shuster, Will Eisner, Bob Kane, Bill Finger, William Moulton Marston, and Steve Ditko. I also owe a debt to the people who are not household names, but who still wrote and drew—and write and draw—comics month after month. That the superhero is ubiquitous is because of all those who created and continue to create their adventures. This goes as well for the people who keep the superhero flame burning in the movies and on TV. Without extensions into those media, superheroes would likely not be the cultural force they are today.

Stan Lee gets doubly thanked, because of the great foreword he wrote. It's rather amazing to have an adult relationship with one's childhood idol. It's even more amazing to have him say nice things about you in print. Thanks, Mr. Lee.

Of course, while you can't judge a book by its cover, you also can't judge a cover by its book. So no matter what you may think of the contents of this tome, I'm sure you'll agree that Mark Bagley did an incredible job designing and drawing the cover, and that Scott Hanna's inking and Tom Smith's coloring were up to the high standards that Mark set.

I'd also like to thank Randy Duncan, Peter Coogan, and Aldo Regalado of the Comics Arts Conference, who were kind enough to ask me to present a chapter from the book at their part of the Comic-Con International in San Diego this past summer. It was great to have feedback from an audience.

Thanks also to copy editor Bruce Cassiday and proofreader Russell Wolinsky for their meticulous work.

Inexpressible thanks and great love go to Blanche, Jim, and Pat Fingeroth for their commitment to this project. Superheroes all, I say.

Thanks to Richard Hyfler, Amelia Rosner, and Robin Groves, who provided me with space to write. Why did I need space? Because my old writing space is now my twin sons' Ethan and Jacob's room. And while they inspire and delight me, it's appropriately hard to research and write when they're around. Your daddy loves you, guys.

Finally, and most significantly, boundless thanks and unending love to my wife, Varda, for putting up with the absences, sometimes even when he's in the same room, the partner of a writer/editor/complainer has to deal with, for giving us the gift of those boys, and for keeping the faith.

D.F.

INDEX

Comic-book and similar characters are alphabetized by first name. Thus, Bruce Wayne under "B" and Lenny Bruce also under "B."